WHERE MEDICINE MEETS MONEY

Why Hospitals Behave The Way They Do & How It Matters

SUDHAKAR JAYARAM

INDIA • SINGAPORE • MALAYSIA

Dedication

For the unsung heroes of healthcare—

Our doctors, nurses, paramedics, and administrators who face difficult choices every day, balancing compassion with efficiency and humanity with business, often at great personal cost.

Especially to that nurse who stays an extra hour to comfort a patient who feels helpless and frightened, to that doctor who dares to care, defying budgets and bureaucracy.

This book is dedicated to your resilience, quiet acts of courage, and the sacrifices you make that few will ever see or acknowledge.

Contents

Acknowledgements

Strange and even weird as it might seem, I want to first acknowledge the metastatic Cancer that devastated me and my body. Without that storm to shake me, I would have drifted through life, bound by unconscious habits and the relentless need to conform. Cancer taught me that not all storms come to disrupt your life, some come to clear your path. The price I paid was steep, but without that, I wouldn't have had the time to self-reflect or find the head space to write this book. It is a shitty disease, and I don't wish it on anyone, but I wish for the grace and mind-space I experience after my battle with it for everyone.

To my friend first and wife-in-arms, Veena, for weaving a protective armor around me during some of the darkest times, allowing me to persevere in my various creative pursuits during almost a decade of tumult.

To my bestie Varun for supporting me with editing and formatting as I struggled with writing due to the severe chemotherapy-induced neuropathy affecting my limbs. To my campus comrade and book buddy M. Vishweshwer (Vishy Garu) for his thorough review and suggestions to make the content flow better.

To my treating physicians and friends, Dr. CB Keshavamurthy, Dr. Neelesh Reddy, and my cousins Vishu (Capt. R. Vishwanathan) and Chuchu (S. Suresh) whose support lifted me when I felt defeated, guiding me through a time when I thought I had reached the end.

To the doctors and nurses, who I am unable to list here due to space constraints, who allowed me access into their "minds" and provided valuable feedback.

Finally, to my beloved Mother and Teacher (AMMA) for instilling the idea that the biggest tragedy in life is not death, but to die without striving and achieving one's fullest potential. To blossom completely...

Preface

Doctors have ceded a lot of space to management and administration, for far too long. We can appreciate that clinical duties are paramount. However, several decisions that directly and indirectly impact patient care plans, safety, and performance get taken many a time without the doctors being adequately involved or designing them. It seems to me that hospital administrators prefer keeping their doctors at the periphery, especially when it comes to economics.

Most Doctors, privately and in smaller groups, continue to rue their almost complete loss of franchise and agency within the hospital system. They have all but accepted enslavement to financial, operations, and administrative leaders by deserting hospital leadership and distancing themselves from key hospital policy matters influencing economics.

The attitude "let management do what they want, and I will just focus on my patients and practice" is probably no longer tenable or sustainable. It is like a person sitting on the branch of a large tree, attending to the leaves and shoots, ignoring others who seem to be working the main trunk of the tree. The risk for the person on the branch atop the tree is much higher! I wonder why doctors don't see this risk.

Unlike in the past, when it was just the doctor and the patient in a "parent-child" relationship, healthcare systems are now incredibly complex. Hospitals are heavily indebted to banks, shareholders, managers, increasingly powerful regulators, and litigious "consumerist" patients. Each one of the above has conflicting agendas with relatively lesser knowledge of medicine or biology of the human anatomy as compared to doctors.

There is also a growing trend towards privatization of healthcare in emerging economies. In markets like India, almost 70% of all care is in the private sector. Even in countries like China, where the state is pervasive, over the last decade, the share of private hospitals has increased from 10-12% to about 40-45%. The USA has a strong network of private hospitals. Fee-for-service payment mechanisms continue to be dominant and contribute close to 70% of the healthcare provided in the USA. One can witness a similar scenario unfolding in parts of the EU. Private equity investors increasingly influence healthcare systems. These investors often operate within a defined 'lifecycle,' requiring an eventual exit strategy to satisfy stakeholders. This process involves significant risk, as promoters and investors may even provide personal guarantees to fund operations. Given the stakes involved, their concerns and anxieties are understandable.

But the balance between economics and medicine is a gentle and delicate one. A balance that can only be maintained with alignment and mutual coordination.

In a largely private system, economics will always be front and center. The risk to doctors is when "good medicine" cedes too much space to "good economics."

The time for doctors to rue and helplessly grumble over their largely self-inflicted disenfranchisement and enslavement is over. They have no choice but to "grab the bull by the horns" to find the sweet spot where "good compromises" between good medicine and good economics can peacefully co-exist.

The Covid pandemic demonstrated to us that doctors must be at the forefront of designing and delivering care. There is nothing that is non-medical about a hospital enterprise.

It is in the doctors' interest and in the interest of their patients that doctors be actively involved in influencing key hospital strategies and policy decisions. Doctors must equip themselves with practical wisdom and tips on hospital economics, strategy, and personal leadership, which most doctors seem to have ignored hitherto.

As CEO of large tertiary and quaternary care hospitals over two and half decades and across geographies, I was involved with designing, commissioning, and, for years, managing hospital enterprises.

One of my biggest 'time sinks' was aligning management, administration, and doctors. After several missteps, I realized I needed to invest time into truly understanding doctors as individuals and 'step into their minds.' Unlike engineers or scientists, doctors often have a different mindset. Discussions about economics for doctors can't be separated from their psyche and mindset. Financial matters and emotional infrastructure are often, inseparable.

I have seen the challenges that doctors face as a CEO and even more closely as a late-stage cancer patient.

I have seen them trying to do the "right thing" for the most part, in a system that has become ridiculously complex.

This book is specially curated for doctors. It is a tribute and expression of gratitude to all those doctors who face what I call "The Great Physician Predicament."

This book is my humble attempt to bridge the often-overlooked gap between medicine and economics—a gap that I've seen challenge doctors, administrators, and entire systems. It's not just a 'fun' handbook; it's a personal journey shaped by real experiences, missteps, and lessons learned. I wanted to understand why the worlds of healing and finance feel so disconnected, and in this book, I offer practical ideas to align goals, foster better understanding, and create real congruence. It's not perfect, but it's honest. Written especially for doctors who juggle the art of medicine with the demands of economics every single day.

This book is not a treatise or a piece of jargon-littered scientific reporting. It comes straight from the gut with the sincere desire to help make doctors' lives easier. If you are dancing between stethoscopes and spreadsheets, this one's for you!

I hope that the content will encourage doctors to reflect and hopefully enable some of them to participate in key strategy and board meetings. I sincerely hope that this "toolkit" will encourage my doctor friends to make the transition from the "Procedure Room" to the "Board Room."

Albeit targeted to doctors, a broader audience, including managers and hospital administrators seeking a career in hospitals, are also likely to benefit from this book.

Section 1 (Chapters 1-4) sets the context. To persuade doctors to divorce the reluctance to lead. Section 2 (Chapters 5-12) provides what I feel are some of the key economic concepts for doctors. These are distilled from my experience of what doctors might need most when dealing with management and bean counters. When they start throwing numbers, you will need more than your stethoscope to survive. I also share my views on things that are wrong with hospital pricing, costing, and current value measurements. Also included is a chapter on Hospital Shopping that might seem a tad controversial, but a trend that I think will gather momentum as pricing models and transparency mature. Section 3 (Chapters 13-15) provides some prescriptive "recommendations" for my doctor friends, as they navigate this crazy and ever-changing landscape. Maybe even learn how not to get punched by economics in the face. Section 4 (Afterthoughts) closes with brief personal views on the impact of AI on medicine and my observations on doctors' attitudes towards economics and lawsuits with prescriptions that tie it back to the topics that are outlined in Section 1.

My long and arduous battle with late-stage cancer gave me the mind space to provide some shape and form to all the notes I had jotted down in an eventful 25+ year career across the globe. I never really thought that these rough notes would become a book someday and me an author.

My purpose in writing this is simple: to connect with you. Yes, I have strong opinions, and I won't shy away from sharing them, but I'm not here to preach. I want to spark thoughts, stir emotions, and take you to the crossroads where 'good compromises' can be found—and reveal dangers that often hide in plain sight. This is not just a book; it's a conversation, and I hope you'll see yourself in it.

I also hope that non-doctors will leaf through this, so they understand their doctors and their situations better. It is important we "step" into each other's heads and shoes. Learn to see the world from another PoV.

I ignored every 'expert' who told me to polish the style, trim the edges, or make this book 'editor-approved.' Why? Because I wanted it to carry my personality—flaws, quirks, and deficiencies. This one's for my doctor friends, not for the grammar police. Frankly, I have little patience for people who claim to be 'experts' and forget that life is about learning, stumbling, and getting better.

So, here's my book—raw, real, and hopefully a fun, adventurous ride. Enjoy the parts you like; I'll forgive you for skipping the rest ☺

Context Changes Everything

(Bloomberg)

Chapter 1

When Conflict crawled out of the Crib

"Medicine is a science of uncertainty and an art of probability." – Sir William Osler

Medicine is a constantly evolving science that seeks to understand and decode the complexities of human beings at every level - physical, emotional, intellectual, and social.

Human bodies, unlike mechanical systems, do not operate predictably. There is so much more we don't know than what we think we might know about ourselves. The proverbial "tip of the iceberg" is a good metaphor for what we understand today about our bodies, brains, and minds. It is therefore fair to say that the human body has to heal itself with some assistance from medicine and healthcare interventions we receive while in a hospital. Hospitals deliver this service of healthcare, which is a business. As a business, they must maintain a delicate balance between Care, Outcomes, and Costs. The balance is important as any hospital setting involves multiple stakeholders with conflicting agendas and objectives.

Let me paraphrase this. "Healing is an art form that lies at the intersection of the science of medicine and the business of delivering healthcare to an entity that responds non-linearly and unpredictably. This art requires both warm-hearted compassion and cold, objective computation in equal measure."

When computation (head) and compassion (heart) intersect and compete for space, it is natural for conflict to emerge and slowly crawl out of the crib. Conflicts lurk at the intersection where "good economics" and "good medicine" jostle for space.

Conflict seems intrinsic to the very fabric of a hospital. I will make this abundantly clear in the upcoming chapters that explain the intrinsic complexity and hybrid nature of hospital systems.

However, let me start with a few forces at work that add sting to this chaotic conflict that is a hospital.

1. Ranging from 52% to 75%, depending on geography, more doctors are part of the employed model[1] working for hospital chains and networks. This proportion is probably higher amongst younger doctors and graduates of medicine beginning their careers.

2. Hospitals and healthcare-related stocks have provided some of the best returns in the stock markets, attracting a lot of institutional funds. Hospitals are growing organically and through mergers and acquisitions. The trend is relentless. The good old days of a family physician practicing independently, who was like our family member, is becoming as rare as a hen's teeth.

3. COVID demonstrated the lengths to which our doctors and medical practitioners go during crises. Several thousands willingly risked and even paid the highest price whilst battling the pandemic to save citizens.

4. Nations go to great extents to safeguard the well-being of their military personnel and their families. We acknowledge and actively celebrate their efforts and lives in our movies and other media outlets. War doesn't happen every day, and not every day is the defense personnel at mortal risk. Doctors and our caregivers, working in hospitals, which are fertile breeding grounds for deadly pathogens, are in harm's way every single day. The dangers they face are mostly invisible and unpredictable. Somehow, this risk, they assume, is inadequately understood and acknowledged.

---

[1] Advisory Board. (2024, April 16). Physician employment trends: PAI and Avalere study findings

5. The growing trend of consumerism will only intensify with the advent and maturation of AI and technology in medicine and healthcare.

6. Over the past two decades, healthcare costs have consistently outpaced the inflation rates of other goods and services. A study reported by Milliman Medical Index found that medical inflation has exceeded general inflation 87% of the time, averaging almost 2.0 percentage points higher than general inflation.

With these and other tectonic shifts in the healthcare landscape, doctors have no choice but to become more actively involved in management and leadership. The conflicts are only bound to intensify, and adopting the strategy of an ostrich is unlikely to be a wise move.

There's another troubling phenomenon in our society that I call the Dehumanization of Doctors. When we face illness—be it acute or chronic—we rush to doctors, unloading onto them our endless physical and mental struggles. In those moments, we elevate them to the status of demigods, placing them on impossible pedestals. Yet, the very next moment, we tear them down, accusing the profession of profiteering and painting doctors as the villains of the piece. This contradictory cycle not only undermines the medical profession but also forgets a simple truth: doctors are human, too. They richly deserve our understanding.

How many times have we paused and reflected on the mental fitness, happiness index, and strains on the minds of our doctors, nurses, and other frontline healthcare workers? Aren't they warriors fighting within the borders to save lives? To improve the quality of our lives?

Unlike many other professions, doctors endure an incredibly long and grueling training period. By the time they finally start practicing and earning a stable income, they're often well into their mid-life, struggling to provide a decent standard of living for their families. On top of this, years of education leave many burdened with heavy debt—a weight that doesn't just sit on their shoulders but deeply affects their psyche. The cost of becoming a doctor isn't just time and money; it's mental and emotional, too.

Their days are extremely crowded with scores of patients needing attention at the OPD, IP rounds, OT procedures, teaching, counseling, MDTs (multi-disciplinary team meetings), administrative duties, and training juniors. It doesn't end when they reach home. Can they turn their mobiles off? They have to be available to deal with emergencies. Many doctors continue to provide consultation on the phone to friends and family members, and they probably don't even get paid for it most times. When I asked a senior doctor about this, he indicated that that was part of the hazard he signed up for when he chose to become a doctor. This is probably true, but is it sustainable?

Don't medical professionals (as warriors within borders) need breaks and pauses? Isn't their physical, mental, financial, intellectual, and spiritual well-being equally, if not more important than that of the general population? Statistics reveal that doctors are not doing too well, both physically and mentally. We will discuss this in the chapter where we take a "peek" into our doctors' lives and minds. Doctors also have families and face similar struggles and aspirations as any of us might face on a day-to-day basis. This perversion of dehumanizing doctors must end. We must, as a society and as individual patients, make an effort to understand and reflect on the state of well-being of our doctors.

A good place to begin a practical study of hospital economics, is by entering into the minds of our doctors and understanding their psyche. Economics might have much to do with that.

Chapter 2

It is a Job!

"When work is framed as a 'calling,' burnout becomes a badge of honor"

Stop calling it a "Calling"!

Is being a doctor just another job? Or is it a Calling? The answer, I guess, depends on who you ask. Likely, that a higher proportion of senior physicians who are well into and above their late fifties might see it as a calling. In contrast, that proportion amongst younger doctors might be a lot lower. This is just based on my observations, and I have no study to back this up. For generations, doctors have been leashed to their pagers, and now those devices have taken many more shapes and forms. It is not uncommon, I think, to find a general sentiment amongst the seniors that the younger lot of doctors don't "sacrifice" as much. I think that the younger doctors are questioning the culture of work that is pervasive in medicine. And I think the youngsters are probably right. Maybe it is a job. A job that must be done well and, indeed, could be a calling for some. This chapter presents a study mostly gleaned from the survey done by Medscape. Calling it a "Calling" may partially explain the survey results, which seem worrisome.

The survey results are sure to surprise a common citizen. They are consistent and resonate with scores of doctors I have personally interviewed across geographies, disciplines, and settings. I strongly believe that efforts must be made to build awareness among common citizens about the challenges of being a doctor. Let us dive into some of the survey results.

Survey Study 1

70% of chief physicians in Germany report that economic pressure and burden they experience negatively impact patient care.[2]

This surprising finding comes from a survey in Germany, which is largely a public healthcare system. One can only imagine the pressure and burden of economics on doctors in private, corporate, and pure fee-for-service systems. This German study also acknowledged economic pressures causing substantial deficits in nursing and human interaction.

If a patient were to ask a doctor: "Is this the right treatment for me?". In today's scenario, sometimes, doctors might find that question difficult to answer with their hands on their hearts. Doctors should never have to face such a dilemma, but it seems likely that they might very well do in the situation that they find themselves in today. I suspect that a significant proportion of doctors, especially in corporate fee-for-service facilities, might privately admit that some patients are over-diagnosed and receive over-treatment.

Sometimes, patients must be turned away as they might not be adequately insured or cannot afford the hospital charges. They are generally referred to government facilities where (especially in emerging economies) lack of attention due to very high volumes can sometimes compromise the quality of care. I know many conscientious doctors who struggle with this humanitarian burden. They know that the outcomes could have been different if economics had allowed it.

---

2 Reifferscheid, P., Morin, P., & Wasem, J. (2014). Umgang mit Mittelknappheit im Krankenhaus. Springer-Verlag.

Survey Study 2

80% of physicians are at full capacity or are overextended. An astonishing 78% experience burn-outs![3]

Burnout among doctors is a "burning" issue that warrants urgent attention. I cannot adequately overemphasize this issue and would like to dwell a bit on this matter, given its serious implications for society.

Doctors are 1.87 times more likely to commit suicide than those working in other professions[4]. We can probably imagine the stressors experienced by a police officer, given the nature of their job. They are 1.54 times more likely to die by suicide. Doctors' suicide rates are 21% higher than those among police officers. 4% of all deaths amongst doctors, after considering all causes, result from suicide. These are studies conducted and published by NIOSH (National Institute of Occupational Safety & Health). Allow that to sink in! Your doctor is likely to be very stressed. Remember this, the next time you talk to her. Some empathy might help both of you.

There is a complex interplay of multiple factors that underlies this burn-out phenomenon:

1. Massive asymmetry between patient load and availability of doctors. For example, the allopathic doctor-to-population ratio in India is around 1:1404. It is way below the WHO norm of 1:1000. Interestingly, 52% of all doctors in India are probably practicing in just five states.

---

[3] Medscape. (2024). Medscape physician lifestyle & burnout report.

[4] Duarte, D., El-Hagrassy, M. M., Couto, T. C. E., Gurgel, W., Fregni, F., & Correa, H. (2020). Physician suicide: A systematic review and meta-analysis. PLOS ONE, 15(12), e0226361.

2. Increasing awareness, access, and insurance coverage. Public spending in healthcare is around 2.1% of GDP for India. It is around 10% in OECD countries. This skew exacerbates the load on private hospitals where most doctors are employed or practice.

3. Increasing patient activism and rampant medico-legal cases

4. Current economic models are such that hospitals and doctors get paid and incentivized to "do more." There doesn't seem to be a sustainable revenue model in preventative health yet. Doing more obviously means less sleep and more stress.

5. Other issues range from lack of control, inequities in the workplace, conflicting demands and priorities of stakeholders, technological disruptions, etc.

Aviation has strict rules that ensure the safety of pilots by ensuring adequate rest and sleep time. FAA (Federal Aviation Administration, USA), for example, mandates that pilots must have a minimum of 10 hours rest before beginning a flight period. Of this, there should be a minimum of 8 hours of uninterrupted sleep. Additionally, pilots are required to have 30 consecutive hours of off-duty in any seven consecutive days. In India, the DGCA has further restrictions such that a pilot cannot have more than 2-night landings, down from 6. An aircraft will not fly even if one cabin crew member is missing or delayed.[5]

Now, contrast this with what happens with our doctors and nurses. When was the last time we enquired if our treating

---

[5] **National Transportation Safety Board (NTSB). Directorate General of Civil Aviation (DGCA).**

doctor or nurse rested and slept well? Does anyone even bother? Our model today makes our doctors sprint the marathon. A bad strategy and a recipe for disaster due to unsustainable levels of stress and burnout. Doctors are not jackrabbits on an endless supply of Red Bull!

Survey Study 3

Less than one-half of all physicians (48%) believe they are fairly compensated for their work, and this has been steadily falling over the years. 52% remain highly dissatisfied![3]

This may come as a surprise to the common citizen, who is generally under the perception that doctors earn rather well and are amongst the wealthiest. Indeed, they are generally well compensated. However, for the hours they log in and the risk they undertake, doctors don't seem to agree. It is certainly a finding that needs examination.

Unlike most other professions, doctors start earning much later. The tuition and preparation process can span over 12 torturously long years after high school. They are already in their mid or late thirties by this time. After this, they must build their "personal brand" and a patient base, which can also take several more years. This is generally not acknowledged or even understood. Debts undertaken during this period also weigh heavily on their minds. Working hours are demanding, and much of that can be non-bedside administrative duties for which the doctors don't get paid separately. Most attend midnight/ weekend on-duty calls that may not be fairly compensated, even if at all. Hospitals are very complex and especially dangerous places, as we will see in the next section. The risk of infection remains clear and present every time a doctor is in the hospital. This daily risk that the doctors assume is taken for granted and probably not adequately factored into their compensation. In the US, orthopedic surgeons topped the list as the highest earners. Followed by cardiologists and radiologists. Primary Care doctors could be earning a lot less. Even amongst tertiary care, a cardiac surgeon may earn several times more than a pediatrician, for example. The choice of discipline, location, population, etc, seems to significantly impact the lifetime earnings for doctors. These factors might help explain why there is a general dissatisfaction amongst doctors with their earnings.

Survey Study 4

46% of the doctors surveyed plan to change career paths. If they could time travel, only a bare majority (51%) of physicians would still choose medicine as a career. Overall, satisfaction with the field of medicine has been steadily declining.[3]

If we exclude the effect of technological advancements, the top 3 professions that have seen the most significant declines in satisfaction are Physicians, Teachers, and Social Workers. This is dangerously worrisome as the foundational pillars of any nation are education and health. With the advent of AI, AGI, Robotics, med-tech advances, etc, some of the disciplines in medicine could be at risk of complete disruption within the next decade or so. How might this impact the decision of medicine as a career choice? These are not trivial questions, and the answers remain unclear.

Survey Study 5

52% of the physicians surveyed indicated that the relationship between themselves and the hospital management/administration was somewhat or mostly negative.[3]

Physicians probably carry the perception that management and administration "live in their ivory towers" and do not adequately understand bedside dynamics. That, management is mainly interested in pursuing financial goals at the expense of patient and physician safety or satisfaction. Unsurprisingly, management may privately hold the view that doctors don't adequately understand the economic nuances and challenges of running a complex hospital business. Both perceptions have merit. How often has a CEO or CFO entered or spent time within the OR (operating room) or OPD (out-patient-department)? Conversely, how often have doctors participated in meetings around budgeting and governance? Alienation between management and physicians is a reality across hospitals and geographies.

Survey Study 6

Ranging From 52% to 70% depending on geographies, more Doctors are part of the Employed Model than the Independent Practitioner model.[3]

Many large private hospitals are funded, owned, and/or run by non-medical professionals. They are measured by and naturally inclined to attend to financial outcomes. This is understandable. It is the fiduciary responsibility of the Boards to fulfill the just financial demands of the investors and shareholders in return for their investments and risk. Doctors must rethink the dilemma and might have no choice but to become more actively involved in management/leadership and positively influence hospital economics.

Doctors may not have been asked to lead or felt the need to be frontline leaders. They probably never fancied themselves as leaders. This probably changed during COVID-19 as doctors became frontline leaders.

Today, hospital services focus primarily on operational metrics like – waits and delays, resource utilization rates, and intervention rates. Management's focus is on the transactions of care delivery. However, as the focus in health care systems increasingly shifts to 'value' and outcomes in health care delivery, clinical leadership becomes more important and hence, doctors should take center-stage.

Doctors unwilling or uninspired to lead organizations focused solely on the efficiency of resource allocation may be more willing to take an active leadership role in those focused on clinical outcomes and value-based care.

Survey Study 7

70% of the doctors surveyed said they would not recommend medicine as a career to their children. This number is increasing.[6]

Amongst all the survey results, this last trend especially caught my attention. It singularly gives us a vivid description of the mindset of today's doctors. Their lives are not easy. As recipients of medical service, we must also contribute positively so that the atomic and sacred interaction between us as patients and our doctors is meaningful and enriching.

I suspect that the issue in referring to medical practice as a "calling" and giving it an almost "religious" spin might be more harmful for both doctors and patients in the final analysis. Doctors like any of us need a healthy work-life balance. Might be better to just treat it like another job, a critical one, no doubt but not add the psychological stress and pressure that comes with making it sound evangelical.

In the next two chapters, I deal with the intrinsic complexity and hazards of a hospital. More reasons for doctors to alter their mindsets and consider an active leadership role. I warned you that I might be a tad persistent! Indulge me...

---

[6] Why 70 percent of physicians would not recommend the profession. (2018). Healthcare Finance News.

Chapter 3

Hospital Complexity? Good Luck, Einstein!

"Medicine is not rocket science. Just tad harder"

Intrinsic Complexity

Healthcare systems are probably among the most complex organizational structures we know of. When we think complex, we tend to think of organizations like NASA or ISRO. However, hospitals can be equally, if not more, complex. This might sound exaggerated to most readers. But in my opinion, not many industries or organizational structures are as complex and unpredictable as hospitals. Complexity is intrinsic and built into the design and fabric of a hospital system.

Complexity in hospital systems originates from an interplay of the six factors native to hospitals. I have listed them below with examples in parentheses:

1. Tight Interconnectedness (between departments)

2. Non-linearity (unexpected patient outcomes)

3. Emergence (unexpected complications/infections)

4. Uncertainty (unclear diagnostics and/or biological responses)

5. Diversity (patient demographics, staff expertise)

6. Scalability (volume and patient load)

This is by no means exhaustive, but it gives us a glimpse into possible and innumerable "failure points" that exist across the system. My intention is not to delve into complexity science but merely to highlight its role in the dynamics of balancing medicine and economics. Let us simplify things a bit. Have a look at Exhibit 3.1, titled "Systemic Complexity"

SYSTEMIC COMPLEXITY

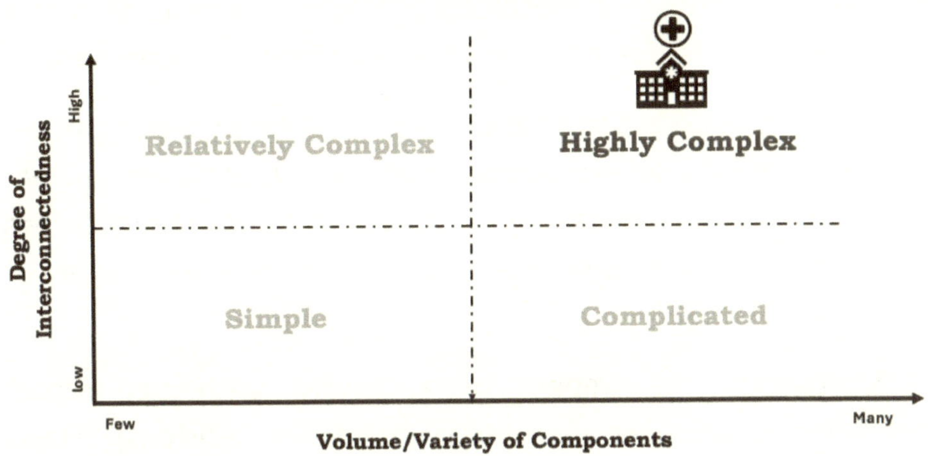

Exhibit 3.1: Hospital fall in the category of highly complex systems

The complexity of any system depends on two key variables:

1. How many components are part of the system, and

2. How interconnected are these components?

Based on these two, we can classify systems falling into four quadrants:

Q1: Few components and little interconnectedness - Simple Systems.

Q2: Many components and little interconnectedness - Complicated systems.

Q3: Few Components and High Interconnectedness - Relatively Complex and

Q4: Many Components and High Interconnectedness – Highly Complex.

If we combine the six factors listed earlier and verify the level of interconnectedness, hospitals fall into Quadrant 4- Highly Complex systems. Let me cite a few examples to illustrate this:

1. Imagine an elderly patient with multiple co-morbidities, suffering a severe condition where protocols are unclear or, at best, iterative, gets afflicted by a hospital-acquired infection and is resistant to most of the known array of antibiotics.

2. Imagine the impact of a flawed pathology report (on surgical or medical intervention decisions). Flaws due to poor maintenance or calibration of laboratory equipment and instrumentation that the reporting doctor might be unaware of.

3. Imagine errors that could creep into the EMR (electronic medical records) or care plans when used by multiple users and inaccuracies generated during hastily done shift handovers.

4. Patients with similar medical conditions don't necessarily respond similarly to the same medication or interventions. Most interventions are standards-based, but disease and biological responses are molecular.

5. There always seems to exist a mismatch between the 'patient in the protocol' and the 'patient in the bed' due to multi-morbidity and interacting sociocultural influences.

Mechanical system behaves linearly. They interact linearly and generally produce results that can be measured and predicted with reasonable accuracy. Additionally, we can generally control the output of a mechanical system by manipulating the input variables.

In contrast, Complex Systems interact non-linearly and can produce unexpected results. The output of a complex system is dynamic, and feedback can vary dramatically with situation and input conditions. Importantly, we have little or no control to manipulate input conditions and variables in a biological system.

A health care system comprises networks of divergent components viz: IPD (in-patient department), OPD clinics, imaging, pathology, nursing care, rehabilitation units, pharma drugs, implants, governments, medico-legal, families, and patients that interact nonlinearly on different scales –

And often produce unintended results and consequences (adverse drug reactions, nosocomial infections, re-hospitalizations, poor functionality, or financial decline both for the provider and recipient of medical services).

Recognition and internalization of the magnitude of this complexity should encourage us to seek adaptive, collaborative, and integrated care models as rational responses. Ideally, incentivize self-reflection and humility. Sadly, this doesn't seem to be the case.

What seems more common, though, is more management interventions and policy changes that generally disintegrate into blame-gaming, finger-pointing, etc. Usually, such interventions seem to worsen the very problems they were introduced to resolve.

Complex systems need not necessarily respond positively to a typical "top-down" and an aggressive "more is better" approach.

Not only are hospitals complex, but they are also hybrid beasts. A Polyplex! Exhibit 3.2 highlights the two key factors that give hospitals their 'Janus-faced' nature. Let's explore each of these factors in detail.

Hybrid Beasts

COMPLEX & HYBRID

Hospitals occupy a financially hybrid position, balancing production and human services imperatives

Process Knowledge Spectrum in Healthcare is characterized by remarkable breadth, depth and complexity

Exhibit 3.2: Hospitals are a Polyplex – Both Hybrid and Complex.

Hospitals are a mashup—part auto repair shop, part luxury hotel, part cafeteria (with questionable food choices), part high-tech science lab, part soap opera, part factory assembly line, and part cruise ship (minus the relaxation). All of this comes together in a cacophony of organized chaos, where every day feels like a reality show with no script.

Additionally, albeit, hospitals are generally classified as a service industry, their financial behavior seems to resemble that of a manufacturing industry.

Most businesses have two types of risks. Business Risk and Financial Risk. Hospitals, like any other business, also have these risks.

The Business Risk of an enterprise, is measured by operating leverage (OL). Higher OL means higher business risk as the component of Fixed Costs is higher relative to overall costs. This is typical of manufacturing companies. A consulting firm, in contrast, has high variable costs and so low OL.

Financial risk is the level of debt in the system and the ability of the enterprise to service the same.

Hospitals are classified as a Service Industry but due to High Fixed Costs (high OL), they exhibit the behavior of a manufacturing enterprise financially! Also, most hospitals are also leveraged due to high levels of debt financing.

Another fascinating characteristic of hospitals that generally goes unnoticed is the breadth, range and variety of services that are delivered within the same facility and ecosystem.

As an example, within the same hospital, it is not uncommon to find a nurse administering a vaccine while in a different area, a doctor is inserting a central line at the ER, which takes him a few minutes. At the same time, one of his senior colleagues might be performing a complex, laparoscopic, or robotic procedure that could take her up to 6-8 hours. I doubt if many other systems make such demands of the process knowledge spectrum as hospitals do of their caregivers.

Exhibit 3.3 attempts to classify into a framework the broad spectrum of process knowledge that is unique but commonplace in hospitals.

Process Knowledge Spectrum

PROCESS KNOWLEDGE SPECTRUM IN HOSPITALS

Modes of Care	Repetitive	Customized/Iterative	Experimental
Decisions/Tasks	Standard/Dichotomous	Validated Heuristics	Untested Heuristics
Example	Diabetes/CVD/CLI	CA Pancreas	Alzheimer's/Lupus/LTC
Nature of Knowledge	Understood/Predictable	Probable/Predictable within a Range	Poorly Understood/Unpredictable
Care Process	Standardized Protocol	Protocol with subroutines	Emergent/highly customized
Clinical Lead Focus	Minimize Variation	Optimize Selection	Discover new solutions
Lead Attention	Systemic	System and Patient	Individual

Exhibit 3.3: Uniquely extensive process Knowledge Spectrum.
Courtesy: The Instrumental Value of Medical Leadership, Prof. Richard Bohmer, The King's Fund

If there was one and only one argument that I was asked to use to persuade doctors to participate and engage actively with and in management/leadership roles, it would be the content in Exhibit 3.3. The basis for the framework was developed by Prof. Richard Bohmer. It encapsulates how current knowledge of a disease condition affects care plans, clinical focus, and diagnostic decisions.

Modes of care based on the disease condition are classified as: 1. Repetitive, 2. Iterative, or 3. Experimental.

1. Repetitive: Disease conditions like cardiovascular (CVD), diabetes, etc where the nature of knowledge is well understood and predictable are classified as Repetitive. The care plans have standard protocols, and the focus is systemic to minimize variation and secure the best outcomes.

2. Iterative: Disease conditions (e.g., cancer of the pancreas) where the nature of knowledge is understood with some degree of uncertainty are classified as Iterative. The standard care plan protocols need some customization with sub-routines for individual patients. Demographics and Psychographics could also have an impact on the care plan design. The focus here is the type of patient and disease. The objective is to optimize the selection of treatment plan and recovery regimen to secure the best possible outcomes given the constraints and challenges surrounding each patient.

3. Experimental: The Experimental group comprises disease conditions (such as Alzheimer's, Lupus, or even Covid) where the nature of knowledge is poorly understood. Care plans must be highly emergent and customized using untested heuristics in some cases.

The modes of care, design of care plans, and the focus of clinical attention vary widely depending on where the patient's disease condition resides within the process knowledge spectrum. This breadth of knowledge required is breathtaking and uncommon in most industries. Further highlighting the complexity native to hospitals. Doctors intimately understand this. I don't think that a fancy suit in finance or an investment banker who might have a seat on the board will be able to understand the nuances of such process knowledge complexity. Doctors ceding too much management space to non-medical professionals under such circumstances is a monumental folly---it undermines the very foundation of effective healthcare leadership. I can understand the concern doctors might have around the trade-offs between being a medical practitioner and being involved in management. Hence, I want to briefly make a distinction between leadership and management. Doctors cannot cede leadership responsibility. Leadership, or the art of providing direction, "doing the right thing". They may consider leaving management ("doing things right") to the experts if practical constraints preclude them.

The contradictory and paradoxical financial behavior of hospitals coupled with the depth of the process care spectrum might make a hospital system seem like a giant hairball of spaghetti difficult to disentangle. As if these twists weren't knotty enough, the system is also assaulted by a mix of stakeholder groups, all jostling for space. Considering their unique roles and quirks, I like to refer to them the *'Hospital Avengers'*. Let us meet them now.

Hospital Avengers

On the face of it, a hospital is meant to accomplish something rather simple and straightforward. A patient with a symptom visits a doctor, and the two of them together decide the best way to remedy the condition. Everything lies at the heart of this atomic interaction between the patient and the physician. However, it can be quite amusing to notice how this simple one-to-one has gotten so complicated. There are so many different stakeholders ("Avengers") in a hospital system with divergent agendas and goals.

POWERFUL STAKEHOLDERS – HOSPITAL AVENGERS

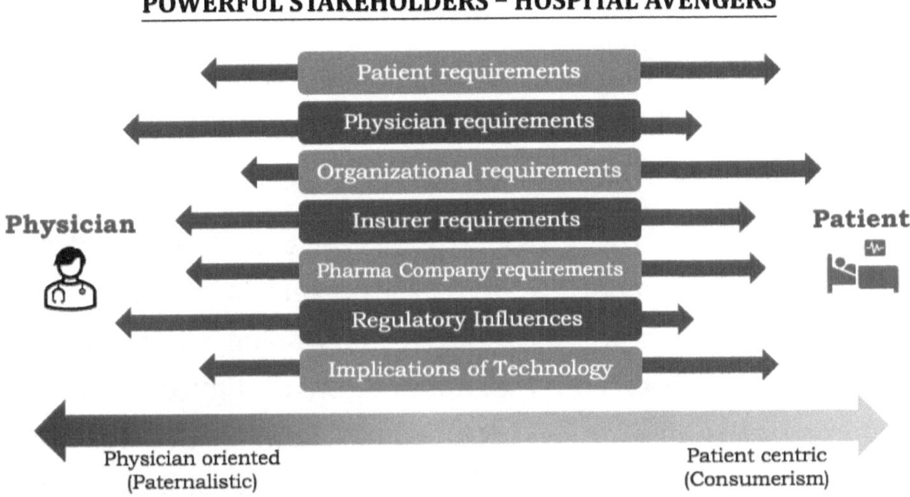

Exhibit 3.4: Powerful Stakeholders and Competing Forces that shape the Physician-Patient interaction

Exhibit 3.4 attempts to depict all the different stakeholder "avenger forces" that heavily influence and shape the nature and sometimes even the result of the interaction between the patient and the physician. Let us examine the priorities of each of these stakeholders and the individual forces they exert on the hospital ecosystem.

1. Patients: They desire optimal therapy, the best outcomes and lowest possible costs.

2. Physicians/Healthcare professionals: They desire optimal therapy, best outcomes, appropriate remuneration, and safety.

3. Governments: They desire securing supply, access and high levels of cost-effectiveness.

4. Health Insurance: They desire lower reimbursements and higher coverage.

5. **Owners/Promoter:** They desire positive returns and a good reputation.

6. **Drug and Pharma:** They have their profit and research-related motives.

A hospital lies at the crossroads of these divergent interest groups and the competing forces they exert. A fertile ground, for conflicts to fester! The relative bargaining power of each of the stakeholders and the application of limited financial resources available to a hospital, determine the resultant hospital "organization design." If not carefully calibrated, the relative power of these forces could lead to hospitals (which are already complex by design) becoming very dangerous places. For example, it is not difficult to imagine a hospital in your town that may wax eloquent on being patient-centric, but you know that it is probably just mere lip service. The organizational design in such a hospital becomes unstable over a period, affecting all parties. Patients and Physicians should always be first, front and center. Reality though is anything but that.

Another visible shift that has most doctors fuming is the transition from Paternalism to Consumerism. Medicine has faced criticism (and understandably) for its history of paternalism. Where the "papa" doctor imposed his view on the "child" patient, who was expected to comply without a murmur. The balance of power though is shifting from the "paternalistic" physician to the patient. This change is largely driven by the increased availability of clinical information on the Internet. "Papa" doctor is not amused. As technology matures, patients or healthcare consumers, as they might call themselves, will exert reverse pressure. Doctors cannot resist technologies like

ChatGPT, Grok, and the scores of AI models in medicine that will become pervasive within the decade.

Consumerism in and democratization of healthcare WILL be a reality. It is a matter of "when" and not "if". How this unfolds and affects the relationship dynamics will be a fascinating study.

Another emerging cartel is the Insurance Companies. As insurance coverage increases worldwide, their power can be significant as they will control both Patient flow and Payment. That might very well be a new form of paternalism, largely invisible to citizens. It will most likely diminish the autonomy of the doctor, hospitals, and probably even the patient. As it seems to me now, there is a trust deficit between citizens and the hospital system (especially when it comes to pricing), and insurance companies could use this gap to shift the landscape in their favor.

I almost forgot to mention the power of regulators, courts, and the influence of citizen action groups and their implications for doctors and hospitals. Especially if hospitals don't start looking closely at their pricing and providing some level of price transparency, I can visualize governments and even the top courts seizing the matter and muddying the waters for large private corporate hospitals. (especially in emerging markets like India)

Because of this, hospitals are utterly dangerous as they are complex and hybrid. Let me share some studies that argue this unambiguously.

Dangerous & Hazardous

Exhibit 3.5 depicts an image of a daring young girl bungee jumping. What might be the connection between this image and hospitals? The answer might surprise you. Statistically, it is safer to bungee jump than to visit a hospital. Do you find that absurd? But numbers don't lie.

HOW DANGEROUS IS A HOSPITAL?

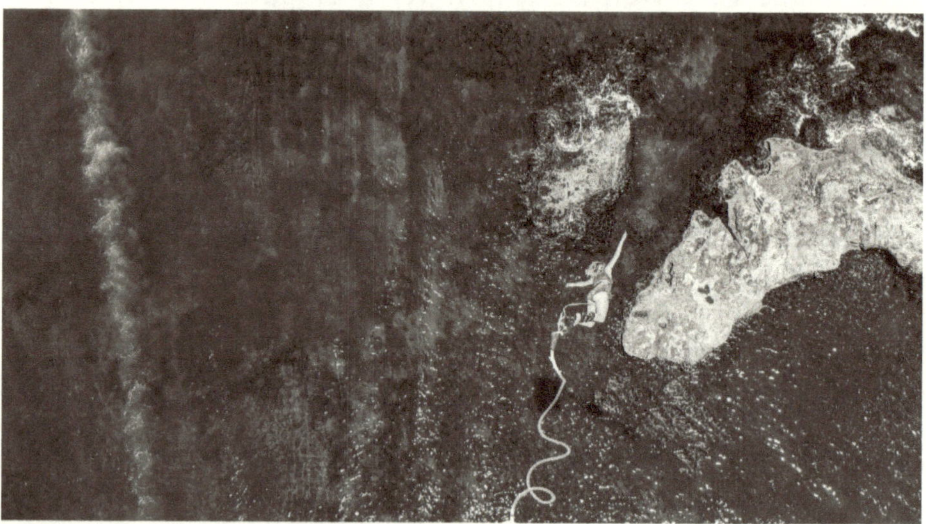

Exhibit 3.5: Bungee Jumping and Hospitals

When faced with a medical condition, we seek medical attention and sometimes might need hospital admission. It is normal to feel safe and relieved once you have been admitted into a hospital under the care of a physician. Hospitals are indeed safe havens as they help us return to our lives. But did it ever cross your mind that they can also be utterly dangerous places? Read on, the irony won't be lost on you!

Have a look at Exhibit 3.6. In this graphic, industries are classified into three buckets:

1. Ultra-Safe 2. Regulated, and 3. Hazardous.

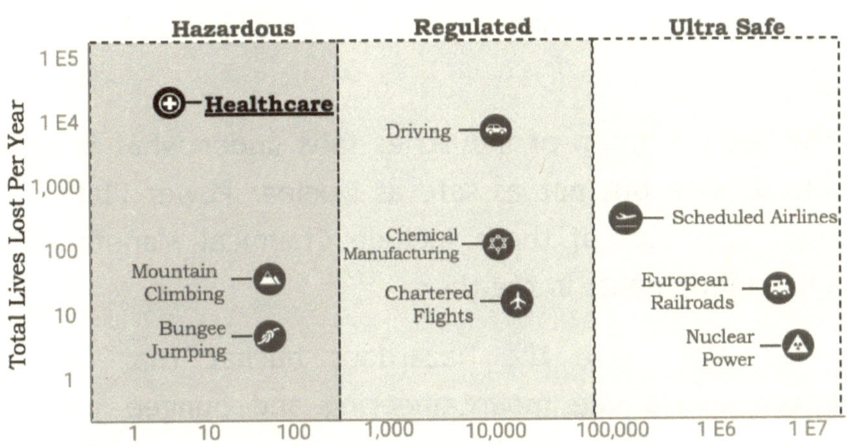

Exhibit 3.6: Hazardous Hospitals.
Courtesy: Harvard University of Public Health

Observe the relationship between the number of encounters before an adverse event or fatality occurs (X-axis) and the annual number of lives lost in these industry segments (Y-axis)

Contrary to popular perception, Nuclear Power Plants rank the safest. Equally safe are European Railroads and Commercial Airlines. All fall under the Ultra-Safe Category. Chernobyl and Fukushima come to mind, and somehow, our minds believe that nuclear power plants are dangerous. They are utterly safe! So are commercial airlines.

As an example, in the decade between 2010-2020, commercial airlines around the world flew about 35 billion miles. US-based airlines alone ferried approximately 7 billion passengers during this decade. The fatality numbers boasted 0.1 deaths for every 15 billion miles flown. The safety records of Nuclear Power Plants and European Railroads are even more impressive than that. Imagine how wrong our perceptions could be!

The second group of industries falls under what is called Regulated. Safe but not as safe as Nuclear Power Plants and Aviation. Examples of these include Chemical Manufacturing and Chartered Flights in the US.

Finally, we have the hazardous bucket that includes adventure sports like mountaineering and bungee jumping. Hospital statistics on safety based on these parameters are worse than those of these dangerous adventure sports. In just one year, 2016, the US reported 251,454 deaths on account of medication error alone[7]. Not including deaths due to CVD, cancer, respiratory, etc. Let that sink in! Based on these statistics, hospitals are astoundingly dangerous places.

According to Exhibit 3.6, an adverse event happens in hospitals for every 250-300 encounters. That technically makes hospitals as or probably more dangerous than bungee jumping! Statistically.

Isn't it strange that there is so much media coverage around the risks of nuclear power plants when, indeed, they have the

---

[7] Makary, M. A., & Daniel, M. (2016). Medical error—the third leading cause of death in the US. BMJ, 353, i2139.

best safety record? When was the last time you heard the media talking about how dangerous was the hospital in your town? Not surprising, I guess, given that the business of media and journalism (these days) seems to be more about entertainment than about uncovering the truth. Also, notice how faulty our intuitions are. Maybe our intuitions are overrated, and our perceptions mostly faulty.

This astonishing safety statistic surrounding hospitals is reiterated by data available even from sources like the WHO[8]. I have highlighted some of them below:

1. Available evidence suggests that, in low-and middle-income countries, there are 134 Million adverse events in Hospitals each year.

2. In low and middle-income countries alone, adverse events in Hospitals contribute to 2.6 million deaths annually due to unsafe care.

3. Patient Harm due to adverse events is among the Top Ten causes of death and disability across the world. This is comparable to malaria and tuberculosis.

4. Across the world, 7 million people a year suffer disabling surgical complications, from which more than 1 million die.

5. Worldwide, there is a 1 in a 300 chance of being harmed whilst accessing healthcare.

---

[8] World Health Organization. (2019). Patient safety: Global action on patient safety.

6. 15% of all hospital spending in Middle-income countries can be attributed to treating patient safety failures, estimated to be several billions of dollars.

Until this point, we have peeked into the minds of our physicians and attempted to understand their challenges. We also got a glimpse into the structural paradoxes and conflicting agendas of participating stakeholders in a hospital ecosystem. I presented arguments on a hospital system's intrinsic complexity and provided evidence of the utterly dangerous safety records of hospitals. My intention is to set the context. With the hope that these arguments would persuade doctors to actively participate and influence their hospital's governance and direction. We need our doctors in the Boardrooms as much as we need them in the Operating Rooms.

...because **"Context Changes Everything"**[9]

We should also remember that exceptionally brilliant minds like Einstein, Tesla or Dirac are not around to help us decode this hospital universe. They appear once in a millennium.

In their absence, we should probably resort to Humility and consider if Less is More!

More on this next.

---

[9] Bloomberg Media. (2022).

Chapter 4

Maybe Less is More!

"In complex systems, control is an illusion. We create order not by imposing control, but by letting go and allowing the system to self-organize."

We are probably conditioned to think that anything complex and difficult demands more management, more regulation, more resources, and invasive governance. There is an undying anxiety to "do more" and intervene when faced with a challenging or complex task. Might we be wrong in this approach? Could less be more?

If we examine complex systems in nature, they seem to be self-governing. They follow simple, practical rules and exhibit a high level of adaptation and emergent teamwork.

It might sound far-fetched, but we can learn lessons from the ant and bee colonies, from the flocking of birds, schooling of fishes, synchronized lighting of fireflies, etc. They seem to self-govern and self-organize themselves. There is no apparent hierarchy. They are also complex systems. Complex systems in nature seem to be emergent.

The starting point is the acknowledgment amongst the various stakeholders that hospitals are complex. That, in a system like healthcare, everything ultimately depends on the "last mile" - the bedside the atomic interaction between the doctor and the patient at the bedside. A sacred interaction that needs to be empowered and enabled. This needs humility and a mindset to adapt and collaborate. Humility allows us to embrace paradoxes. Accept dissent and disagreements. Critically examine our assumptions and always remain skeptical of our methods and processes.

Unfortunately, many of the stakeholders in the healthcare ecosystem seem to be blind to this intrinsic complexity. Each of these "avenger" stakeholders is confident, probably even over-confident that the other stakeholder is wrong. We have "eyes", but we are unable to "see". Nobel Laureate Prof. Daniel Kahneman once famously said: "Not only are we blind; we are also blind to our blindness[10]."

However, if health care is uniformly viewed as complex, then several of its intrinsic properties can be exploited to influence its dynamic behavior. We can maneuver it in a more favorable direction. Nature teaches us that complex systems are self-organized, emergent, and based on simple rules. Such natural systems seem to be successful and harmonious.

Maybe the way to govern complex systems is not the way we govern other systems, which is a typical top-down hierarchical approach. Complex systems have porous boundaries. They constantly adapt, adopt, and evolve with other sub-systems. Intrinsic variables and components operate based on rules that are not clearly defined or adequately understood. Maybe we should attempt to enable and accentuate this intrinsic property of complex systems. Fortunately, there are some real-world examples we can turn to for inspiration.

Model 1: Self-Management Organization

(Example: Morning Star Company[11])

Morning Star, based out of California, is a tomato processing company. Founded in 1970, this company operates without

---

10 Kahneman, D. (2011). Thinking, fast and slow. Farrar, Straus and Giroux.

11 Hamel, G. (2013). The Morning Star Company: Self-management at work (Case No. 914-013). Harvard Business School

traditional managers and hierarchy. There are no job titles. Employees manage themselves, making decisions and taking responsibility. Employees set personal annual goals. Conflicts are resolved via a peer-mediated process. The company has close to US $ 700 million in revenues.

Model 2: Flat Organization

(Example: Valve Corporation[12])

Valve is a gaming software company with a flat organizational structure. Again, there is no traditional hierarchy or managers. Employees choose projects and work autonomously. Employees allocate company resources with complete transparency in financials. Decisions are distributed with regular feedback loops.

Model 3: Podular Organization

(Example: Amazon[13])

Amazon, the Bezos behemoth, follows a podular structure. This enables autonomy and innovation. Podular teams are self-contained with clear objectives and goals. At the top of this cluster is the "S Team," a small group of senior executives reporting directly to the CEO. This structure allows for clear lines of authority and efficient decision-making processes,

---

[12] BBC. (2013, September 23). Valve: How going boss-free empowers staff.
[13] Research-Methodology. Amazon organizational structure: A brief overview.

which are crucial for a company of Amazon's size and scope. Amazon has adopted a service-oriented architecture (SOA) to enhance scalability and efficiency. This architectural approach allows individual teams to own their codebase and functionality, fostering rapid development. We have seen the innovation of customer satisfaction combined with efficiency and scalability that Amazon has managed via this model.

There are probably many more examples. Some of them might sound a bit fancy and even impractical at first. However, unless we fundamentally alter our way of thinking about hospital management, I doubt things will ever improve.

There are valuable lessons from Amazon, Morning Star, and other innovators that hospital systems can borrow and allow for greater autonomy in the "trenches." This also means greater participation of doctors trained in the basics of economics and leadership. Management should also learn to get out of the way, occasionally. The results can be pleasantly surprising.

In conclusion, I want to emphasize the development of a 'systems mindset.' One that might help us recognize the changing interdependencies between sub-systems. This need not resolve the inherent contradictions and tensions within the system, but it will allow us to negotiate good compromises and build creative solutions. A complex system demands a lot of empowerment and continuous training in the trenches (and at the bedside).

Dear reader, if you have been with me so far, I would like to recommend a 4-pronged strategy. It might not resolve all your challenges but might equip you to take up the cudgels more confidently in steering the direction of your hospital. Here are your 4 prescriptions:

1. Understand Key Components of Hospital Economics

2. Understand the Hospital Swiss Cheese

3. Maximize Vacation and Personal Time and

4. Implement Mindset Shift

This book deals with hospital economics. I will share my Prescriptions 2-4 later in this book (Section 3). We get to business now (Section 2) and discuss my views on hospital economics. I admit that economics and numbers can be boring for many doctors. A place where excitement and enthusiasm go to die, you may think. There is no way I can mitigate this. That is why I invested all this effort so far, to "seduce" you into the boring but fascinating stuff that is buried in the chapters ahead.

Hospital Economics 101

Chapter 5

The Holy Grail: Revenues, Costs, and Profitability

"Revenue is Vanity, Profit is Sanity,
Cash is Reality and Cash is King."

Revenue Cycle & Profitability

When a company draws up a specific project plan, financial analysts estimate the RoI (return on investment) for that project. This is based on a business plan. To be profitable, all projects must generate a Return on their Investments (RoI) greater than their Weighted Average Cost of Capital (WACC). For ongoing operations, managements look at several other metrics, such as RoS (return on sales), RoA (return on assets), and EBITDA (earnings before interest taxes, depreciation, and amortization). RoS provides us with a glimpse into the Profit & Loss behavior, while RoA gives us a view into asset utilization efficiency and the strength of a Balance Sheet.

Exhibit 5.1 will provide us with a guided tour of the revenue cycle for a hospital operation. I have simplified it for illustration.

HOSPITAL REVENUE CYCLE

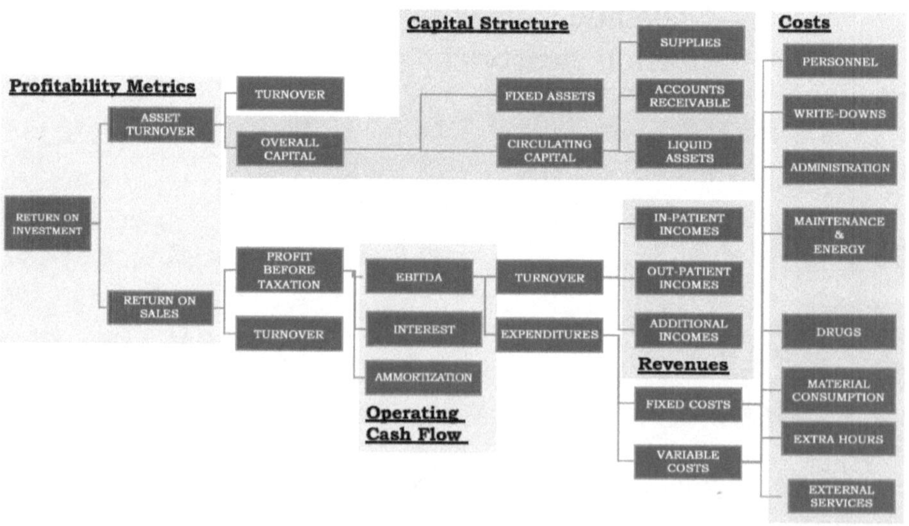

Exhibit 5.1: The Holy Grail - Revenues, Costs and Profitability

We will travel from the right to the left of the exhibit. First, we traverse the RoS cycle at the bottom half and then the RoA cycle at the top.

Costs are broadly of two types. Variable and Fixed. Variable costs are so-called because they vary with business volume. In hospitals, they refer to materials, drugs etc. More patients mean these costs will also increase.

You have other costs that are fixed. Doesn't matter what the level of OPD, IPD, or ICU (intensive-care-unit) numbers there are certain fixed costs and overheads (admin costs, maintenance, staff, etc) that remain the same.

We can further dissect these costs into costs that can be directly associated with or traced to individual patients and costs that are indirect. This way, we have four cost sub-categories:

1. Variable-Direct,

2. Fixed-Direct,

3. Variable-Indirect and

4. Fixed-Indirect costs.

At this time, just keep in mind that it is mainly the variable-direct costs that play a meaningful role in actual cost control and measurement efforts. We will visit this later in the chapter on Costs and Costing in hospitals.

These two costs add up to provide us with the Overall Expenditure. Accountants also refer to this as COGS (or Cost of Goods Sold).

Hospital Revenues are generated in the form of IP (in-patient) revenues, OP (out-patient) revenues, and others. Depending on the type of hospital and location, one may find that OP and ER (emergency) revenues may vary significantly. Pharmacy, OR, and ICUs contribute significantly to revenues in a tertiary care hospital. There also seems to be a strong correlation between the level/complexity of care delivered and the profitability/ revenues of a hospital enterprise.

EBITDA is the net of overall revenues from overall expenditures as shown in Exhibit 5.1. EBITDA shows how much money an enterprise makes from its core business operations. Hence, it is an especially important metric. It stands for Earnings before Interest, taxes, depreciation, and amortization.

EBITDA is used a lot by analysts and economists because this metric helps compare companies with different capital structures, tax rates, and asset bases. Also, it highlights the core business performance and is a strong cash flow indicator. Investment bankers use this to estimate hospital valuations. One level below EBITDA is PBT. PBT (or Profit Before Taxation) is the proceeds after you deduct Interest and other liabilities from EBITDA. PBT, when divided by Overall Revenues (or Turnover), gives you RoS or Return on Sales.

RoS measures profitability from sales, indicating how efficiently a company converts its CAPITAL inputs into productive sales and captures value in its net income. This is the P&L side of the business and is tracked monthly or quarterly.

On the top are some of the typical Balance Sheet items that include fixed capital/assets. These include plants, machinery, medical equipment, etc. Working or circulating capital includes inventory, cash, accounts receivable, etc. These two (fixed and working capital) together constitute a company's overall capital.

PBT, when divided by overall assets/capital, gives us RoA or Return on Assets, the counterpart of RoS. This metric gives us a view of profitability based on how well the hospital enterprise is utilizing its assets and allocating its resources.

RoS and RoA are used to evaluate company-wide performance. In comparison, RoI is used to assess specific investments in projects. It examines the gains in the quantum of investment in the project. Occupancy and ALOS (average length of stay) are two other metrics that management looks at closely amongst others. There is a reason for it.

In Tertiary and Quaternary care hospitals, one might notice that the bulk of patient billing and revenues happen upfront. So, the first few days are bulked up with all the investigations, procedures, and other surgeries followed by a brief stay in the ICU.

After that, the patient is generally in the ward under observation, awaiting discharge. During this time, the patient is mostly paying room rent, etc. Hence, hospitals also look at ALOS (average length of stay) so that they can turn around their beds faster and improve throughout. However, in their enthusiasm to make more revenue, they must also guard against a discharged patient being readmitted from complications. These are some of the areas where the balance between good medicine and good economics comes into focus. Other metrics like ARPOB (average revenue per operating bed) are also used to review a hospital's operational/financial performance.

Revenue Structure and Behavior

Let us now briefly look at the revenue and cost structures of a typical tertiary care hospital. (the figures are illustrative only and might have an emerging market slant).

REVENUE STRUCTURE AND BEHAVIOR

REVENUE STRUCTURE	% OF REVENUE
Diagnostics	22%
IP-BED	14%
IP-ICU & OT	24%
OP&ER	6%
Pharma	31%
Canteen/Parking	3%

Exhibit 5.2: Pharma, OR+ICU and Diagnostics account for bulk of the revenue in a typical tertiary care hospital. Reference purposes only, numbers could vary

Exhibit 5.2 depicts the revenue structure for a typical tertiary care hospital. These numbers are only indicative and could change between regions/locations and the nature of hospital services. The purpose is to give the reader a glimpse into how various service lines contribute to the overall revenues of a typical hospital. Almost every dollar of revenues that accrue to the hospital is due to the doctors. They decide when to admit, what diagnostics to order, what meds to prescribe, when to transfer, discharge and follow up. Even the innocuous Canteen and Parking revenues is also due to the doctors. Why would I visit a hospital and pay for parking and eat at the cafeteria if not for meeting or consulting a doctor? Doctors should remember this undeniable fact. Let us get back to the revenue line items.

As is evident, the Top 3 sources of revenue are:

1. Pharma @ ~ 31%,

2. OR/ICU @ ~ 24%, and

3. Diagnostics @ ~ 22%

Between them, the Top 3 service lines account for almost 75% of all revenues. The profit margins from these revenue sources are also relatively higher. It is, therefore, no surprise that management maintains a vigilant focus on these three service lines.

This is typical for referral tertiary care hospitals because much of the patient footfalls (probably close to 60%) are via referrals from other primary and secondary centers. ER (~30%) and Walk-Ins (~10%) account for the rest of the patient volume. This explains the reason why large tertiary care hospitals go to great extents to keep their referring doctors in the region "happy". The tactics some hospitals employ to "encourage" primary care doctors and GPs to refer patients to them could inspire a dark comedy series on Netflix, blending elements of horror and humor. Some hospitals also court ambulance drivers and pharmacists with all kinds of goodies and treats to ensure that ailing patients who have little "voice" are "dropped" to their doorstep. Only in the hospital industry does the patient (the consumer who pays) seem to have little to no choice in the services and goods they are made to consume. We will examine this issue of "induced demand" and knowledge asymmetry in Chapter 10, where I share my perspectives on Healthcare Shopping.

Let us now examine the cost structure of a typical tertiary care system. See Exhibit 5.3

Cost Structure and Behavior

COST STRUCTURE AND BEHAVIOR

COST STRUCTURE	% OF REVENUE
Professional Cost (Doctors' Salaries+ Benefits)	22-24%
Staff/Personnel Cost	18-22%
Material Cost	18-20%
Pharma Cost	18-20%
Admin & Operative Cost	12-14%
Marketing Cost	0.8-1.2%
Others	0.5-0.8%

Exhibit 5.3: Doctors' costs account for around 24% of revenues for a well-run tertiary care hospital. For reference purposes only, numbers could vary

The exhibit depicts the key cost components that are the source and the support for the revenue lines we saw in Exhibit 5.2. As is evident, the Professional Costs (which is the cost of doctors' salary and benefits) as a percentage of overall revenue is between 22-24%.

All other payroll costs, including that of nurses and admin staff, would be around 18-22%. The total payroll costs for a reasonably well-run hospital would probably be around 45-55% of the overall revenue of the hospital. Costs of materials and drugs, add another 20-22%. Administrative and other costs account for the rest.

Please note that doctors drive almost 100% of the revenues while occupying only 22-24% of the costs associated with that revenue. In a typical services industry, however, these professional costs would be much higher. But we know that hospitals are janus-faced. Looks like 'services" but behaves like a production enterprise financially. However, in my opinion, there is money that is left on the table that doctors could take home with better negotiation and an understanding of hospital economics.

Another not-so-obvious inference from Exhibit 5.3 is that the bulk of the total costs "seem" Variable. Theoretically, the staff costs, materials, and pharma costs, which are about 70%, might seem like costs that can be adjusted to demand. However, we all know that this is not possible to do in hospitals. So, in practice, it is generally only the materials and pharmacy costs (about 30%) that might truly qualify as Variable. Even here, there are certain limitations.

In hospitals, what appears as a variable, behaves like a Fixed or Semi-Fixed in the short to medium term. This makes hospitals a Fixed Cost Beast, and administrators must deal with what I refer to as the Persistent Fixed Cost Dilemma.

The economics of a hospital that delivers health services behaves more like a manufacturing industry. The added debt that most hospitals take on (in what could be a poorly designed capital structure) adds to the drama that unfolds during a typical day at a hospital. We will examine Capital Structure next in Chapter 9. For now, we will take a quick look at how capital costs generally get applied when starting a new hospital.

Exhibit 5.4 showcases how capital costs are applied when a new hospital is being designed and commissioned.

Capital Cost Structure and Behavior

CAPITAL COST STRUCTURE AND BEHAVIOR

FIXED/CAPITAL COST STRUCTURE	% OF FIXED/CAPITAL COSTS
Land	10%-15%
Building + (CMPEI* etc)	30-40%
Medical Equipment	30-40%
Pre-Operative Expenses	10-15%
Margin Money (Start Up Expenses, Cash Losses, Others)	10%
Contingency	5-10%

Exhibit 5.4: Greenfield Tertiary Care Hospital Capital Costs
*Civil, Mechanical, Plumbing, Electrical, Instrumentation. For reference purposes only, numbers could vary

Land is an issue as real estate prices in India and emerging economies have a massive impact on project viability. Typically, for hospital projects to be viable, it is desirable to ensure that land costs are contained under 15% of overall project costs. However, these costs can exceed 30% and can single-handedly put projects at risk.

Medical Equipment, Building including Fittings and Land, each account for approximately 30% of the overall project cost. (Rough Estimates)

The above three items occupy close to 90% of the capital cost deployment in a greenfield hospital project. Much of these fixed costs and their implications on operations are sometimes not visible to doctors and managers during day-to-day operations. Some of the fixed costs can also become "sunk" over time. These numbers I state are indicative and only to give a flavor to the reader. The actual ratios and numbers can vary quite wildly depending on the nature, size and location of the hospital project.

Many entrepreneur doctors ask me how much it would cost to set up a hospital. It is a fair question but not straightforward to answer. Costs vary widely depending on whether the doctor sets up a primary, secondary, or tertiary. Also, the location, size and other variables play a big role. I have tried to outline this via a compendium framework in Exhibit 5.5 [14]

---

[14] Author Notes. This is only a reference and can vary widely depending on the city, type, size, and medical program of the hospital. Applies mainly to emerging economies. All amounts in USD.

CAPITAL COST PER BED*

FACILITY TYPE (BEDS)	LARGE CITIES	MEDIUM CITIES	SMALL CITIES
Tertiary Care (200-400)	$125K-$210K	$110K-$150K	$70K-$100K
Secondary Care (100-200)	$85K-$105K	$70K-$90K	$50K-$80K
Primary Care (Investment Per Center)	$500,000	$350,000	$200,000

Exhibit 5.5: Approximate overall Cost of setting up a hospital. Per Bed Numbers (USD).
*For reference purposes only, not accurate

The exhibit attempts to consolidate all the costs above and translate them into what it would cost per bed to set up a hospital, considering a few variables.

The next chapter gives you a flavor of Capital Structure. It might feel and taste like Capital Punishment, but the chapters after that aren't as onerous. I promise. Hang in there!

Chapter 6

Capital Structure

"A big business starts small, but a poorly structured business doesn't start at all."

Capital Components

A wise man once said: "Where you end up in life mostly depends on where you start." This is just plain truth. This absolutely applies to Capital Structure decisions. If not attended to and designed scientifically, it can be equivalent to Capital Punishment in the medium to long term. But, I have always wondered, with some frustration and amazement, about the poverty of attention that founders/promoters of hospitals provide to this crucial starting point in business.

A good capital structure ensures that the available funds are used effectively. It prevents over or under-capitalization and helps the company increase its profits in the form of higher returns to stakeholders.

Debt and Equity are the two primary types of capital sources for a business. Capital structure is defined as the combination of equity and debt that is put into use by a company to finance the overall operations of the company and for its growth and sustainability. Another area that receives even scantier attention is adequate Working Capital Planning and Budgeting. Working capital management involves overseeing a company's short-term assets and liabilities to ensure sufficient liquidity for ongoing operations. We will examine this in greater detail towards the end of the chapter. For now, let us turn our attention to the overall capital structure. I cannot help but be a tad didactic in introducing this principle, so bear with me.

Exhibit 6.1 outlines the different types of funds that are raised by a firm. These include preference shares, equity shares, retained earnings, long-term loans, etc.

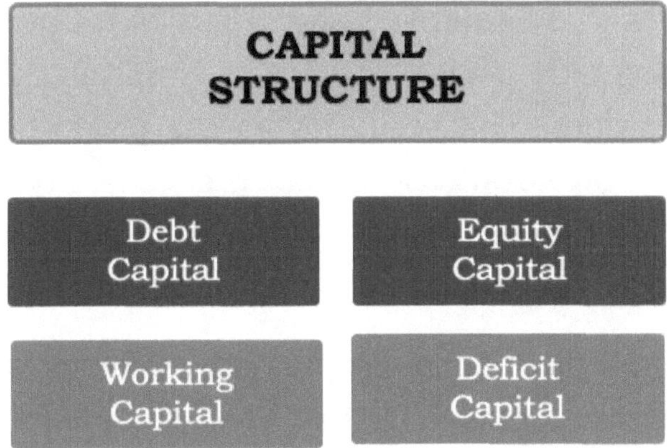

Exhibit 6.1: Components of Capital Structure

Optimal capital structure is the perfect mix of debt and equity financing that helps maximize the value of a company in the market while at the same time minimizing its cost of capital.

Business Risk and Financial Risk

If any of my reader doctors plan on starting a hospital, here are a few simplified prescriptions to keep in mind:

1. There are two types of economic risks that a hospital faces. Business Risk and Financial Risk.

2. Business risk can be defined/expressed as Operating Leverage (OL)[15] and assessed by the level of fixed costs

---

[15] Operating leverage is a financial concept that measures the proportion of fixed costs in a company's cost structure. It indicates how a change in sales volume will affect a company's operating income due to the presence of fixed costs in its operations. The higher the operating leverage, the more a company's profits can increase with additional sales because fixed costs remain constant as sales increase. A tertiary care hospital with high operating leverage will see a more significant impact on profitability from changes in patient volume. If patient volume increases, the hospital can spread its fixed costs over a larger number of patients, potentially increasing profitability.

in the business relative to contribution[16]. One of the ways to measure it is $OL = \dfrac{Contribution}{EBIT}$. Hospitals are generally high business risk scenarios as the proportion of fixed costs in the total cost structure is generally higher than most service industries. We will examine this fixed cost dilemma that hospitals face in the next chapter.

3. Financial risk can be expressed as Financial Leverage (FL) and is assessed by the level of debt in the capital structure. One of the ways to measure it is $FL = \dfrac{EBIT}{EBT}$ or by measuring the debt service coverage ratio.

4. The Total Risk[17] can be measured as OL X FL. So, the $Total\ Risk = \dfrac{Contribution}{EBT}$. Operating leverage measures the sensitivity of operating income (EBIT) to changes in sales, while financial leverage assesses the impact of interest expenses on earnings. The combined effect, often referred to as combined leverage, indicates how changes in sales will affect earnings per share (EPS).

5. Higher business risk projects should follow low financial risk (more equity) and vice versa. More equity is required for projects having higher risk-reward ratios. More debt can be tolerated for projects having lower risk-reward profiles.

6. It is important to synchronize cash flows associated with the capital structure design with the estimated cash

---

[16] In the context of operating leverage and business risk, contribution refers to the contribution margin, which is the amount remaining from sales revenue after deducting variable costs. This margin contributes to covering fixed costs and generating profit.

[17] Operating Leverage (OL): OL = Contribution Margin / EBIT. Financial Leverage (FL): FL = EBIT / EBT. Combined Leverage (CL): CL = OL × FL = Contribution Margin / EBT

flow signature of the hospital project. Debt has typical covenants on liquidity, security, and serviceability. Debt could have maturities ranging from 5-15 years.

7. Equity is the costliest form of financing. Investors typically demand a high IRR (internal rate of return). The higher the perceived risk, the higher the return demanded. Normally, green-field projects have a higher required return compared to brownfield projects with positive EBITDA.

8. Working capital management is often ignored, leading to considerable distress during operations. It must be carefully planned and budgeted.

9. Designing and deploying a scientific capital structure improves investor confidence and demonstrates a company's commitment to financial stability. Deviations in capital structure can lead to increased risk, affecting creditworthiness and investor confidence.

10. Effectively managing investor expectations and addressing factors like currency fluctuations are equally critical components in designing a robust capital structure.

Exhibit 6.2 attempts to capture the above-simplified prescriptions. In summary, the mix of equity and debt is dependent on the perceived/assessed business and financial risk of the business.

BUSINESS AND FINANCIAL RISK

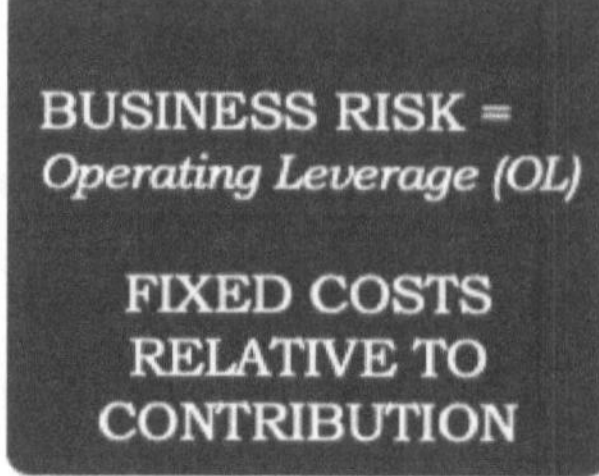

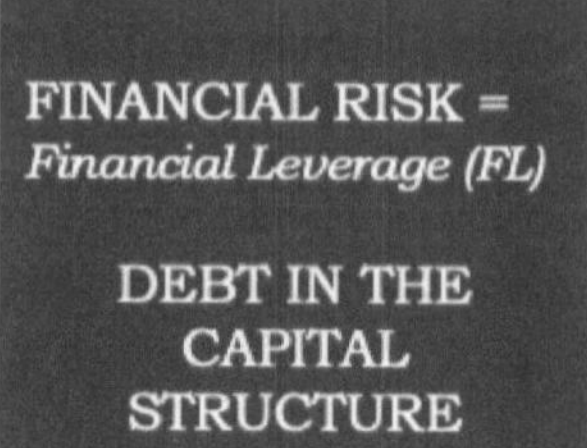

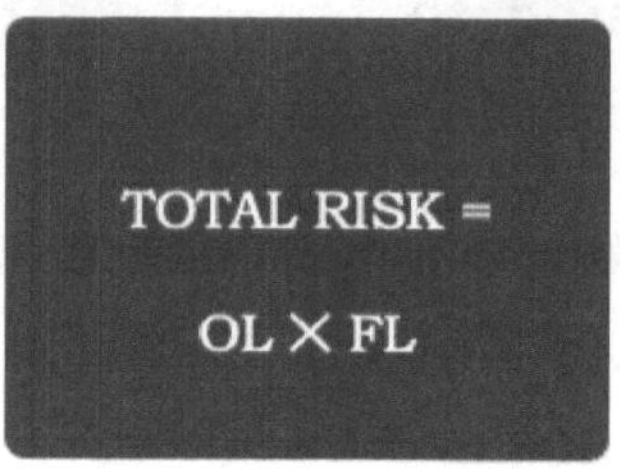

Exhibit 6.2: Business/Financial risk influences mix of equity and debt.

Let us now turn to the orphan child of capital structure design - Working Capital.

The Case for Working Capital – "The Orphan Child"

Another key area where mistakes are made, is the lack of adequate working capital planning and deficit financing. Due to this, in the first few years, many hospitals face significant cash flow problems, causing significant challenges to management and operations.

There is a much stronger relationship between Liquidity ratios and Profitability for hospitals than we might imagine, especially as compared to typical industries. This relationship is opposite to what is observed in typical industries where the correlation between high liquidity and profitability ratios could be negative. This has implications for capital structure and leverage for hospitals as it is a high business and high financial risk operation. Empirical studies[18] show that more profitable hospitals paid their suppliers faster, whereas less profitable hospitals waited longer to pay their bills. Hospitals that collected revenues faster showed higher profit margins than hospitals that have larger balances of accounts receivable outstanding.

In conclusion, a hospital with a sound capital structure has a higher chance of increasing the market price of the shares and securities that it possesses. It leads to higher valuations in the markets.

A Cautionary Tale when Starting a Hospital

Hospital facility designs often proceed with minimal input from CEOs, boards, and medical staff. Typically, architects receive a general brief and create a standardized box, leaving healthcare professionals to adapt to these designs long-term. There are studies[19] that have examined the impact of clinician involvement in hospital boards on the implementation and success of quality management systems across OECD countries. But doctors have

---

[18] Rauscher, S., & Wheeler, J. R. C. (2012). The importance of working capital management for hospital profitability. Rauscher, S., & Wheeler, J. R. C. (2012). The importance of working capital management for hospital profitability: Evidence from bond-issuing, not-for-profit U.S. hospitals. Health Care Management Review, 37(4), 339–346.

[19] Veronesi, G., Kirkpatrick, I., & Vallascas, F. (2013). Clinicians on the board: What difference does it make? BMC Health Services Research, 13, 424.

been kept at the periphery of these critical decisions for the most part.

When we look at the overall lifecycle cost of a hospital project, the cost of maintenance is probably in the range of 80-85%, whereas the cost of initial design in the overall scheme of things is probably less than 10%. Doctors must be deeply involved with the design of the facilities and ensure that functionality and maintenance-related practicalities are not compromised at the altar of some romantic vision of the architect. This is also connected to capital structure, albeit indirectly. Involving clinicians in hospital design is essential for creating functional and efficient healthcare environments. Nurses, for instance, provide invaluable insights that can lead to better patient care and staff satisfaction. Ignoring the insights of those who operate within these spaces daily can lead to designs that are aesthetically pleasing but functionally flawed. Don't let the tail wag the dog!

Finally, Computing WACC (weighted average cost of capital):

Computing WACC

One of the goals of an optimum capital structure is to minimize the overall cost of capital. Exhibit 6.3 below gives you the steps involved in calculating the WACC for your project. This is the hurdle rate to beat.

The Weighted Average Cost of Capital (WACC) represents a company's average cost of financing, considering both debt and equity, each weighted by its proportion in the overall capital structure. Let us imagine a scenario, wherein the hospital project you intend to start requires a total capital (TC) of $100 million, with $40 million in equity (EC) and $60 million in debt (BC).

WEIGHTED AVERAGE COST OF CAPITAL (WACC)*

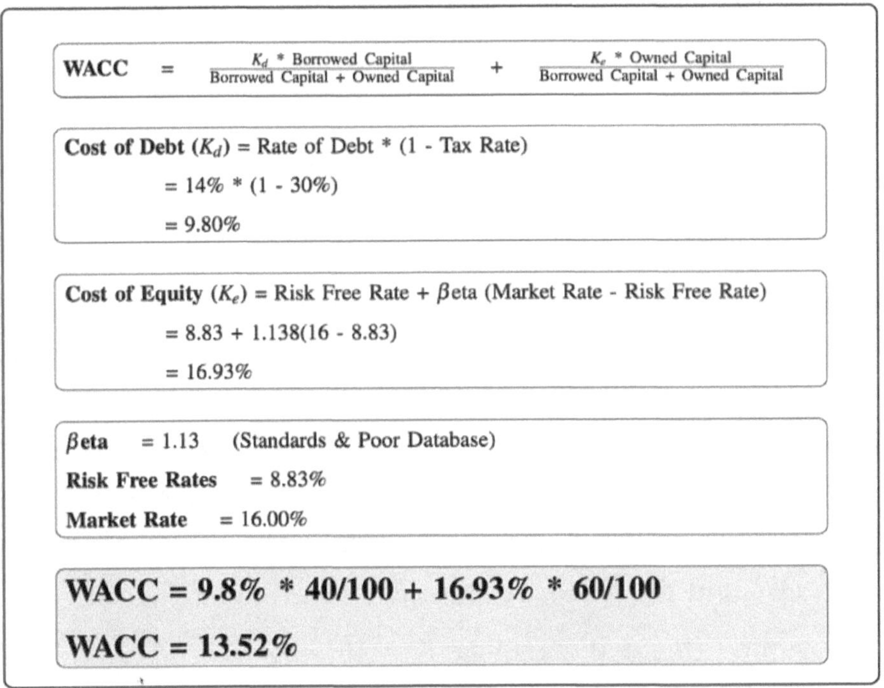

Exhibt 6.3: *WACC Computation. For Illustration and example purposes only.

With this mix, let us see what your WACC will be.

The cost of debt or K_d is the $\text{Rate of Debt} * (1 - \text{tax rate})$ So if K_d is, say, 14%, which includes the rate the bank charges and includes all other fees, commissions, and other expenses related to closing the loan facility. And say tax rate is 30%, the net Cost of Debt is 14% * (1 − 30%) = 9.8%

There is also a cost of the equity. Equity is much costlier than debt but sometimes is not taken into account when we calculate profit in our statements. However, we must account for the same.

The formula for the cost of equity or K_e[20] is $R_f + Beta\left(M_r - R_f\right)$. Where R_f is a risk-free rate, which is what the promoter could have gotten had he/she invested in risk-free govt bonds or with the central bank and other AAA-certified instruments. Beta (β) is the measure of volatility or systemic risk. A measure of 1 indicates that the local markets, as compared to global markets, are in line. A measure of <1 indicates relatively lower volatility, and >1 is higher volatility as compared to movements in global markets. These can be computed and are available in various standard databases that are regularly updated. M_r *is* the expected market return rate. $\left(M_r - R_f\right)$ represents the additional return expected from holding a risky market portfolio instead of risk-free assets. It's calculated as the difference between the expected market return (M_r) and the risk-free rate (R_f).

Based on this, we calculate K_e = 16.93%

So, the total WACC is $\left(K_d * \dfrac{BC}{TC} + K_e * \dfrac{EC}{TC}\right)$, which in this example is $\left(19.8\% * \dfrac{40}{100} + 16.93 * \dfrac{60}{100}\right)$

WACC = 13.52%.

So, our RoI, which we deliver from our operations, must be > WACC to generate and deliver economic profits!

Chapter 7

The Fixed Cost Dilemma

"Fixed costs are like gravity: they always pull you down unless you find a way to counteract them."

Businesses incur both fixed and variable costs while conducting operations. Fixed costs are normally independent of a company's specific business activities. Variable costs increase as production rises and decrease as production falls. Understanding the behavioral differences between these fixed and variable costs and their implications for strategy allows businesses to effectively manage their operations, margins and remain fiscally solvent.

Albeit there are fixed and variable costs in healthcare, the reality is that a significant percentage of a hospital's costs are fixed expenditures associated with buildings, salaries, equipment rent, property tax, insurance, facility maintenance and depreciation, and other overheads. Even seemingly variable costs in a hospital behave as fixed expenses in the medium term. This creates a real problem for hospital administrators. Unlike a traditional services business that can alter operations associated with fixed costs or manipulate their variable costs based on demand, hospitals are severely constrained in their ability to do so. Consequently, hospitals are stuck between a rock and a hard place. The high fixed-to-variable costs ratio creates a liability for hospitals when they are faced with reduced admissions. There is a growing chorus for early detection and preventative healthcare. Governments and Regulators are focused on reducing the healthcare expenditure to balance their budgets. However, (in my opinion) hospitals are not financially designed to deal with such a scenario yet.

The reality is that our healthcare system is designed for "sick-care". Our health systems are not financially designed to keep citizens healthy. This is the stark reality and the naked truth!

Healthier communities mean fewer patients. Fewer patients represent lesser variable costs but also lesser revenues. The ratio of fixed to variable costs in hospitals are such that the burden of fixed costs far outweighs any cost reductions on account of fewer patients. The depressed revenue is nearly not enough to meet the fixed costs of running the hospital, leading the hospital into financial distress.

Widening Revenue Base

Let me illustrate this using a simplified example. Doctors will immediately see the dilemma that hospital administrators face.

Example Illustrating the Hospital Fixed Cost Dilemma:

Imagine a Tertiary Care hospital that has the following numbers (all in USD):

1. Fixed Costs - $ 6.7Mn

2. Variable Costs - $ 3000/patient

3. Average Fee Received - $10000/patient

Let us examine the profitability implications of the three scenarios described below:

- **Scenario 1 – Patient Throughput ~ 1000 (baseline)**
- **Scenario 2 – Patient Throughput ~ 1200 (+20%)**
- **Scenario 3 – Patient Throughput ~ 800 (-20%)**

Exhibit 7.1 outlines the Gross Margin implications for each scenario.

HOSPITAL'S FIXED COST DILEMMA

SCENARIOS	SCENARIO 1 (BASELINE): 1000	SCENARIO 2: (UP 20%) 1200	SCENARIO 3: (DOWN 20%) 800
Fixed Costs ($)	6.7M	6.7M	6.7M
Variable Costs/ Patient($)	3000	3000	3000
Payment / Patient ($)	10000	10000	10000
Patient Load	1000	1200	800
Total Costs ($)	(6.7M + 3000x1000) = 9.7M	(6.7M + 3000 x 1200) = 10.3M	(6.7M + 3000 x 800) = 9.1M
Revenue($)	10000 x 1000 = 10M	10000 x 1200 = 12M	10000 x 800 = 8M
Gross Margin ($)	0.3M = 3%	1.7M = 14%	- 1.1M = -13%
Fixed Cost/Total Cost	6.7M / 9.7M = 69%	6.7M / 10.3M= 65%	6.7M / 9.7M = 74%
Variable Cost/Total Cost	3M/ 9.7M = 31%	3.6M / 10.3M= 35%	3M/ 9.7M = 26%

Exhibit 7.1: A **20%** change in patient volume from baseline swung the gross margins by almost **466%**

Note that in Scenario 2, when the hospital, due to an optimized medical strategy, increases the patient load to 1200, the Gross Margin jumps from 3% to 14%. A 466% jump! However, when the patient load depletes to 800, the Gross Margin dips to a dramatic -13% loss. The hospital goes deep into the red.

A small change in patient volume results in the hospital going from black to red. This behavior is typical of manufacturing and fixed-cost heavy industries where OL (operating leverage) is high. Meaning high business risk.

Hospitals have no incentive today to keep populations healthy. It gains only when citizens have a sentinel event. Hospitals and Doctors get paid for "doing more." Overdiagnosis and Overtreatment are the likely results, consequently frustrating patients and governments alike on the spiraling costs of healthcare. The only way for hospitals today to remain profitable and solvent is to increase patient volume so that the fixed costs are spread over a larger patient base.

Hospitals are forced to "sweat" the equipment and infrastructure. Turn things around quickly and move more caseloads through their beds and equipment. The expensive CT, MRI machines depreciate rapidly, and maintenance costs start adding up. They have to be kept busy 24x7. What is the way around this dilemma? Is there a system that has figured this out. Look no further than Aravind.

Beating Fixed Costs: The Aravind Way

Hospital pricing has been spiraling[21]. It has been at 2X the rate of inflation for decades. Is there a way hospitals can remain profitable, beat the fixed cost dilemma, and yet keep prices reined in?

The legendary Aravind Eye Care System provides us with some clues.

Started in 1976 by Dr. Govindappa Venkataswamy, Aravind[22] is probably the largest and most renowned eye care provider globally. Aravind has performed over 9.4 million surgeries as on date. The system handles close to 3.5 million outpatients annually. Importantly, their commitment to accessible eye-care ensures that many patients receive high-quality treatment regardless of their ability to pay.

---

[21] Ho, V., & Jenkins, D. (2024, October 21). Hospital price increases since 2000 outpaced inflation by more than double, Baker Institute report says. Rice University's Baker Institute for Public Policy.
[22] "Our Story":Aravind Eye Care System.

They have understood that the only way to beat the fixed costs is to Widen the Revenue Base.

They are utterly affordable and have some of the best clinical outcomes for a mind-boggling volume.

Listed below are some of the key measures Aravind has been able to implement:

1. Forcefully Drive Down Fixed Costs by Increasing Productivity ~ 1000+ procedures per day performed across Aravind facilities.

2. Inspired by McDonald's – standardizing delivery at high volumes

3. Hyper Utilization of OTs – Multiple Tables and Nursing Teams

4. Doctors focus on diagnosis & surgery. Elevate Nurses to do the rest.

5. Reuse equipment. >1 patient in an OR. Elevate technicians

6. Over 9.4 million surgeries performed. Almost does what the entire NHS does for eye care for the population of the UK.

Here is their secret sauce: The Aravind nursing team serves as the backbone of their operations. Nurses are meticulously trained and empowered to undertake tasks beyond traditional roles. Nurses administer pre-operative anesthesia, allowing doctors to concentrate on diagnosis and surgery. Additionally, the Mid-Level Ophthalmic Personnel (MLOPs), primarily women recruited from local communities, who receive extensive training to support various aspects of eye care delivery, play a crucial role in ensuring high-quality patient care at scale. By elevating the responsibilities of nurses and technicians, Aravind has created a highly efficient, scalable, and patient-centered approach to eye care.

The hyper-utilization of OT's is another unique phenomenon.

Aravind has OTs that have two or more tables with multiple equipment and instrumentation. A surgeon performs a procedure on one table and then swings the microscope to the other table to perform the next surgery. As this happens, the nursing unit prepares the earlier and/or next table with the next patient. This way, an average surgeon at Aravind performs over 2000 eye surgeries in a year. That is an average of 8-10 procedures per day per surgeon! See Exhibit 7.2

KEY ARAVIND METRICS - IMPACT OF OT UTILIZATION

	Scenario A: One patient in the operating room at a time	Scenario B: Two patients in the operating room at any given time
Surgeon	1	1
Tables	1	2
Scrub Nurses	1	2
Instrument Sets	1	6
Surgeries per hour	1	6-8

Exhibit 7.2: Hyper Utilization of OT. Courtesy: Aravind Eye Care System, Royal College of Opthalmology, Cataract Surgery Guidlines

I'm not sure if this is limited only to eye surgeries or can be extended to other procedures in multi-specialty tertiary care hospitals. However, the phenomenon is worth studying and examining. They keep costs low, quality super-high, and the company highly profitable. Exhibits 7.3 and 7.4 provide evidence of the quality and cost efficiencies that Aravind is able to generate.

KEY ARAVIND METRICS - QUALITY INDICATORS

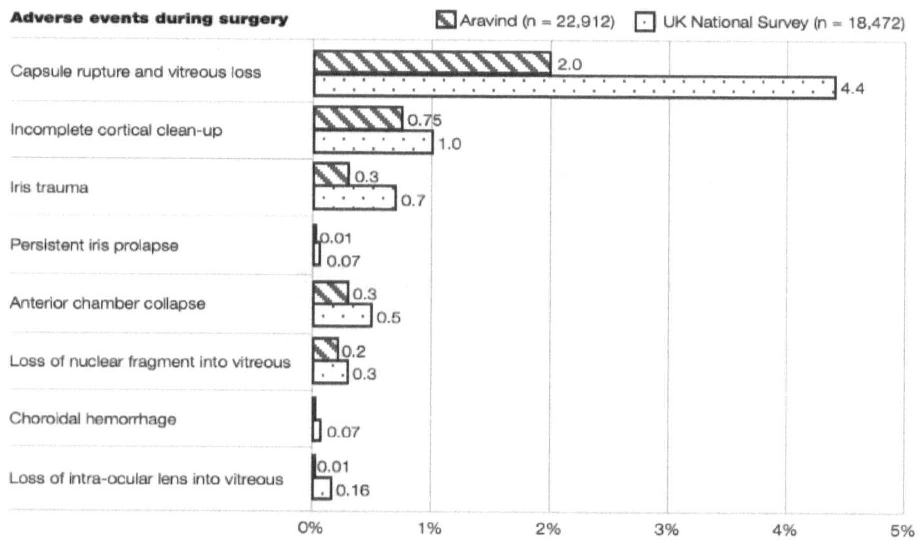

Exhibit 7.3: Complication Rates
Sources: Aravind Eye Care System; Royal College of Ophthalmology, Cataract Surgery Guidelines, February 2001

ARAVIND – PROCEDURE ECONOMICS

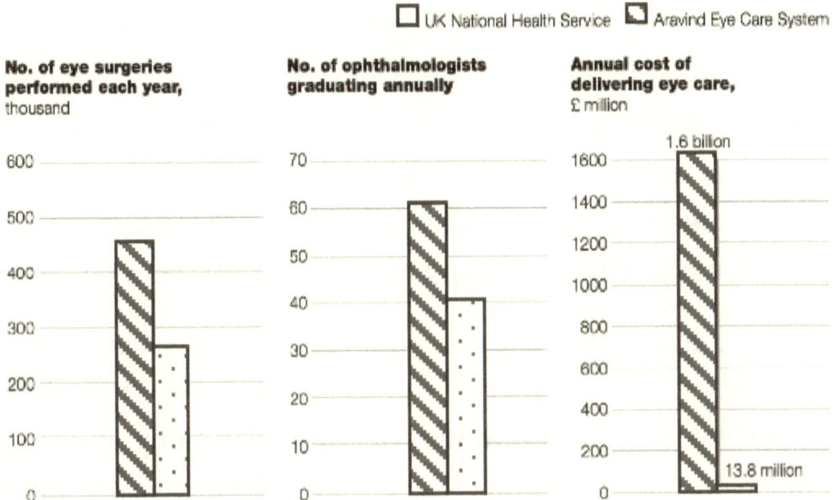

Exhibit 7.4: Courtesy: Aravind Eye Care System; Royal College of Ophthalmology, Cataract Surgery Guidelines

When speaking to a senior physician at Aravind, I understood a basic philosophy. Doctors remain mainly focused on diagnosis and treatment plans. Nurses and Technicians perform a lot of tasks we might see doctors doing in other health systems.

Most private hospitals in India and other markets, keep marking up prices and sneaking additional costs into patient bills to increase revenue. Indeed, input fixed and variable costs in healthcare have steadily gone up over the years. But ultimately, hospitals will be limited in how much they can charge patients because insurers are in the mix, limiting payouts and becoming more powerful. Also, the rampant mergers in the private sector in hospitals are probably partially driven by this need to spread the fixed costs across a larger revenue base. Such mergers can eventually provide significant bargaining power to such hospitals, which can then manipulate both patient flow and pricing. Hospitals have been known to inflate itemized charges, leading to some truly bizarre bills. Mostly driven by the underlying fixed cost burden and the need to beat the hurdle rate and provide returns to shareholders. All this is understandable, but there needs to be some method to the madness. We will discuss this in greater detail when we look at Hospital Pricing (No Method to the Madness). Hospital Costs and Costing are coming up next.

Closely examining and drawing lessons from Aravind might help provide clues into managing hospital systems of the future. It is a shame that someone like Dr. Govindaswamy Venkatappa was not decorated with the Bharat Ratna by any government in India. What a Himalayan contribution to society!

Chapter 8

Until Hospital Costs Do Us Apart

"The hospital bill is often the second shock after the diagnosis."

Primitive Costing Measures

We looked at hospital costs through the lens of a hospital administrator or CFO. Let us examine how patients, doctors, and industry observers generally feel about hospital costs. Listed below are some of my observations.

1. Dissatisfied patients grumbling over bills at the time of discharge is a common sight in many private hospitals. There is a general perception that hospital costing is mired in chaos and veiled in secrecy.

2. Participants in the health care system do not even agree on what they mean by costs. Patients and insurers feel cheated when the final bill seems disproportionately higher than the initial estimates provided. When a hospital talks about its costs, does it mean costs of delivery or costs on patient bills and other invoices?

3. Sophisticated cost accounting systems commonplace in other industries are generally absent in hospitals.

4. There seems to be a constant tug-of-war between insurance companies and hospitals. Payers want to reduce payouts to hospitals. They don't seem to believe the costs charged by hospitals are fair or are based on scientific cost management principles. In some hospitals (in emerging markets), if you are insured, you might find the bills vastly different than if you were willing to pay out-of-pocket.

5. It seems as if some departments and services are always subsidizing others. Some key departments' P&L[23] statements such as those of Endocrinology, Pediatrics, and a few others always seem dismal in comparison to others.

6. Hospitals seem to be generously reimbursed for some services, and pricing reimbursements for some others seem ridiculously loss-making. Especially with government insurance schemes.

Having listed some of the common observations around the general perception of hospital costing, I would like to present my arguments that might shed light on the underlying causes of these issues.

a. Hospitals seem unable to link costs to process improvements. This prevents them from making systemic and sustainable cost reductions. There also seems to be an inability to measure and allocate costs scientifically, which precludes their ability to compare costs with outcomes (both financial and clinical).

b. Also, hospitals don't focus on the costs of treating individual patients with specific medical conditions over their full cycle of care. Instead, providers aggregate and analyze costs at the specialty or service department level. This probably makes certain department P&Ls look more dismal than it is.

---

[23] Profit & Loss

When the hospital is looked at as individual units, some departments seem more profitable and highly revenue-generating than others. For example, an Endocrinologist, a Neurologist, a Pediatrician, or a Renal Physician (key disciplines for hospitals) might not "seem" to generate as much revenue or profits as let us say, a Cardiac Surgeon or an Orthopedic. For example, the lab and diagnostic revenues prescribed by a general physician can be significant. However, these revenues are sometimes not apportioned to the departments, but the cost of all fixed assets is assigned equally, making some departments look less profitable when that might not be the case. Let me explain this with an example of a rehab center. Patients generally take more time at the rehab (so longer ALOS-average length of stay) but don't demand as much attention as in an acute care facility. However, the support fixed costs allocated to rehab may follow the same method as it follows for an acute care facility. This complicates things and causes dissatisfaction among physicians because their compensation is affected. I also think that this anomaly drives a wedge between medicine and surgical departments. And increases conflict between doctors and the administration. There is most likely an invisible "turf war" between medicine and surgery and between doctors, even within the same general discipline.

Due to such costing anomalies, hospitals tend to destroy overall value by focusing on highly paying/reimbursed services and celebrating/compensating some physicians more than others. This introduces major distortions in the supply and efficiency of care.

Hospital Costing seems like a place where math goes to die! A mysterious place mired in chaos and veiled in secrecy. But doctors and their idiosyncrasies also many a time cause costs to go up for no good reason. Let us briefly look at how personal preferences of doctors could play a significant role in cost variation.

Clinical Variability

Another controversial yet relevant subject that has a large impact on hospital costing is Clinical Variability. It is the impact of doctors' preferences and style of delivering care on costs. Therefore, on profitability.

Two different clinicians could treat a similar patient with a similar condition in widely different ways. This is an issue where costs are significantly altered due to a physician's personal preferences that have no bearing on outcomes. This variation is large, persistent, and difficult to measure. It has absolutely nothing to do with the patient's condition or safety concerns. Just plain doctor-led idiosyncrasy. Clinical variation cannot be explained by professional uncertainty on care plans and outcomes but by different behavioral styles or approaches of Clinicians. One argument is that physicians behave as either 'cowboys' (preference for aggressive medical interventions) or as 'comforters' (preference for more conservative actions) based on their judgment of different clinical scenarios and personalities. This basic style has a huge implication on outcomes and costs which is not measured or captured.

Exhibit 8.1 captures a study on clinical variation within the same department at a teaching hospital in the U.K.

CLINICAL VARIABILITY

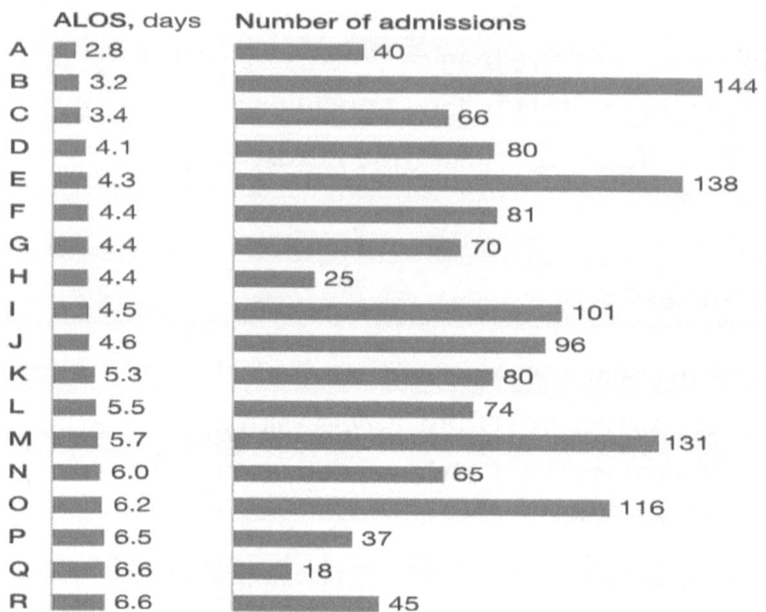

Variation in average length of stay (ALOS) for patients of doctors (A through R) in one department of an English teaching hospital

Exhibit 8.1: Impact of Clinical Variability on Costs. Courtesy: NHS, HES. McKinsey Analysis

The variation in ALOS (average length of stay) between Dr. A and Dr. R is 2.8 days to 6.6 days. A variation of 135%. Patient condition and preferences alone cannot explain this wide variability between these 18 doctors. It has something to do with the "style" of the doctors.

Another milestone study in this area was done by Dr. Kilic et al.[24] Costs of CABG (coronary artery bypass grafting) were compared across 633 hospitals that had performed isolated CABGs in 183,973 patients. Significant baseline variability

---

[24] Kilic, A., Acker, M. A., Gleason, T. G., Sultan, I., Vemulapalli, S., Thibault, D., & Kilic, A. (2019). Clinical outcomes of mitral valve reoperations in the United States: an analysis of the Society of Thoracic Surgeons National Database. The Annals of thoracic surgery, 107(3), 754-759

in in-patient costs was observed after a comprehensive risk adjustment. The average cost of providing the CABG procedure service at the hospital level was $40,424. The SD (standard deviation) of average CABG costs between hospitals was $12,130. A 30% variation! This variation was due to wide divergence in care-pathways adopted by different surgeons to deliver care across the hospital centres. Kilic argues that there is an urgent need to examine these divergent pathways adopted by doctors as outcomes were similar, but costs to the patients and system were dramatically different. High-quality care with positive outcomes is the cornerstone of any hospital enterprise. However, these outcomes must also be delivered efficiently and cost-effectively.

Understanding variability represents an opportunity for standardizing care and improving resource utilization. Clinicians and surgeons must find a way to balance lowering costs, decreasing variability, and improving outcomes. One possible way to address this is by training clinicians on the practice of "Reflective Medicine". A deliberate and objective mindset that is strong on System 2/DTP (deliberate thinking process). Prescription No. 3 which I recommend in Chapter 15. As far as I'm personally concerned, I always remain wary and suspicious of the "cowboy" clinician.

We will now examine the general costing methods used by hospital administrators. This may give us a clue into why most of the so-called cost control efforts are generally an illusion. The savings never seem to show up on the bottom-line.

Costing Methods in Vogue

Costing methods are in continuous evolution, and some are better than others. However, practicality and ease of implementation are also factors that need to be considered. Some of the most popular ones are listed and briefly explained below:

1. **TCS** - The Total Cost of Stay method is easy and straightforward. Its ease of implementation means it is widely used. It is also easily understood, applied, and requires less financial investment. But it can result in lower accuracy.

2. **ABC** - Activity Based Costing assigns costs to specific patient services, treatments, and activities. Activities and resources involved are considered for costing, and the indirect costs are tracked and allocated individually. Although more accurate, this method requires time from managers and significant expenses for implementation and maintenance.

3. **CCR** – Cost-to-Charge Ratio is a Costing method specific to the health sector and does not require significant expenses or managerial time. It is a costing method that allocates costs to patients, services, or departments based on the ratio of actual costs to charges. Accuracy is modest at best.

4. **Economic Costing** - Although not a direct method to develop overall costing, financial analysts sometimes insist on including opportunity costs to differentiate between accounting profit and economic profit. This method

requires careful assessment of opportunity costs, and some costs that do not appear in accounting are included.

5. **RVS** - The Resource-Based Relative Value Scale method assigns a relative value to each service or procedure based on resources required for delivery. It is based on the complexity of the procedure, the quantum of resources consumed, and time duration. It is generally more accurate but can be cumbersome to implement. Its main drawback is subjectivity and inability to reflect changes in process, workflow, and technology. Can be widely used when there are demands on purchases of new and expensive medical equipment.

6. **TDABC** – Time Dependent Activity Based Costing. This method is particularly used to measure detailed costs of specific procedures or clinical conditions along a full cycle of treatment (long term). It is an extension of ABC with the added dimension of Time.

In my opinion, TDABC must be the preferred mode of developing Hospital Costing. Admittedly, it is cumbersome and even practically difficult, but the investment in this effort can return rich dividends and real insights into efficiencies and outcome improvements. This method also provides the most accurate costing picture to hospital management among all methods available. This is based on the work done by Prof. Michael Porter and published in the Harvard Business Review[25]. It provides a practical step-by-step approach to conducting a TDABC study

---

[25] Kaplan, R. S., & Witkowski, M. L. (2014). Using time-driven activity-based costing to identify value-improvement opportunities in healthcare. Journal of Healthcare Management, 59(6), 399–413.

in hospitals. I strongly recommend googling and accessing this seminal work by Porter.

We will end this chapter on Costing by reviewing the cost control challenges that hospitals face and why these measures in hospitals generally don't work.

The Illusion of Cost Control

Cost Control measures seem pervasive and aggressively pursued by hospital administrators. But actual savings rarely seem to make it to the hospital's bottom line or show up in reduced spending and improved profitability. It is presented and argued vigorously in boardrooms, but I wonder if anyone really believes it.

Other businesses around the world have made QI (Quality Improvement) their core strategy. This has generally resulted in vastly improved products and services but also lower costs and increased operating efficiencies. However, similar efforts in healthcare don't seem to generate the same outcomes. Cost containment and cost efficiencies remain elusive. The main reason I believe is the use of not-so-sophisticated costing methodologies. TDABC[26] has the best chance of providing real cost savings but is cumbersome and most hospitals understandably are just plain lazy to attempt it. But there is another reason why cost control measures are useless...doctors aren't adequately involved in the exercise.

---

[26] Institute for Strategy and Competitiveness. Measure outcomes & cost for every patient. Harvard Business School.

I hypothesize that hospital administration attempts cost control efforts without adequately consulting or involving the doctors. Let me illustrate this with some anecdotal evidence by way of a study conducted at the University of Miami and Brown in 2011.

Their cost control program was astonishingly straightforward. Simple scripted weekly announcements were provided to doctors on the number of tests prescribed and the total costs of tests. That was it! The study was conducted over 12 weeks.

At the start of the program, the average daily cost of blood tests per patient was around $147.73. At the end of the program, that had dropped to around $107.84. A spectacular 27% drop. Almost $55000 was saved in the 12 weeks. This meant that, Doctors, when provided with data, determined to eliminate tests that weren't adding clear clinical value. The study unambiguously demonstrates the value of getting physicians involved. Imagine the possibilities of what can happen by merely involving and giving physicians information that they normally might not have! Additional studies confirming such behavior have also been published in JAMA[27].

In another similar study[28], changes in doctors' prescribing behavior were noticed by simply providing doctors posts/messages on different costs of similarly effective antibiotics. The

[27] Feldman, L. S., Shihab, H. M., Thiemann, D., Yeh, H. C., Ardolino, M., Mandell, S., & Brotman, D. J. (2013). Impact of providing fee data on laboratory test ordering: A controlled clinical trial. *JAMA Internal Medicine, 173*(10), 903–908.

[28] Mann School of Pharmacy and Pharmaceutical Sciences. USC study reveals strategy to save $70 million in health care. University of Southern California.

upshot was clear. Doctors almost always did the right thing and reduced costs without compromising on outcomes. I'm personally convinced that all QA (Quality Assurance) and cost control measures will find fruition if doctors are actively and adequately involved. But the attitude in private-corporate hospitals is to keep doctors away from anything to do with costs, or pricing or economics in general. It is indeed ironic. Your MVP (most valuable player), your doctor, is not even in the playing XI when it comes to cost control. Good luck getting anywhere with cost control.

Another reason I think cost control is elusive is that the Overhead Cost allocation is a "black box." To me, it seems more mysterious than understanding the quantum physics around a black hole. Admittedly cumbersome, but these highly paid finance guys in hospitals must do way better than the "peanut butter spread" approach to overhead costing.

I am pessimistic that hospital costing would see any improvements or sophistication in the short to medium term. But here are a few thoughts for the finance guys in hospitals to consider:

1. Focus on Variable Direct Costs. That is generally where the savings are most likely.

2. Overhead allocation must find a better method than just a "peanut butter" approach to spread it across.

3. The cost of hospital spending probably won't come down. However, we might be able to significantly reduce wastage and the rate of increase in cost inflation.

4. Finally, if one cannot or is disinclined to do any of the above, at least, Actively Involve and Engage the Doctor. Trust me, finance executives, however hotshot you guys might be with degrees from fancy MBA colleges, you cannot even dream to do what a doctor can accomplish in reducing and controlling costs and improving outcomes at the same time!

Chapter 9

Pricing-No Method to the Madness

"The biggest driver of hospital pricing is whatever the hospital can get away with."

Some of you might have watched the movie Inception. I had to see it twice to get all the nuances that Christopher Nolan was attempting to communicate. The only thing more confusing than the plot of the movie Inception Is Hospital Pricing. There is no doubt in my mind that pricing in hospitals is arbitrary. It is a movie without a plot or a script. Don't take my word for it. Here is an anecdote from an article in WSJ[29].

The article outlines the costs for a C-section within the Sutter Health Network in California. The costs within the network were reported as follows:

- **Hospital 1: $6,241.**
- **Hospital 2: $29,257.**
- **Hospital 3: $38,264.**
- **Hospital 4: $60,584.**

These are actual figures. Imagine the range and difference from just around US $6K to US $60K! A 10X difference.

On reviewing additional literature, I found more evidence, which has been captured in Exhibit[30] 9.1

---

[29] Appleby, J. (2021, February 10). How much does a C-section cost at one hospital? Anywhere from $6,241 to $60,584. The Wall Street Journal.
[30] Mathews, A. W., McGinty, T., & Evans, M. (2021, February 10). How much does a C-section cost? The Wall Street Journal. Feb 11, 2021

PRICING VARIATION-NO METHOD TO THE MADNESS?

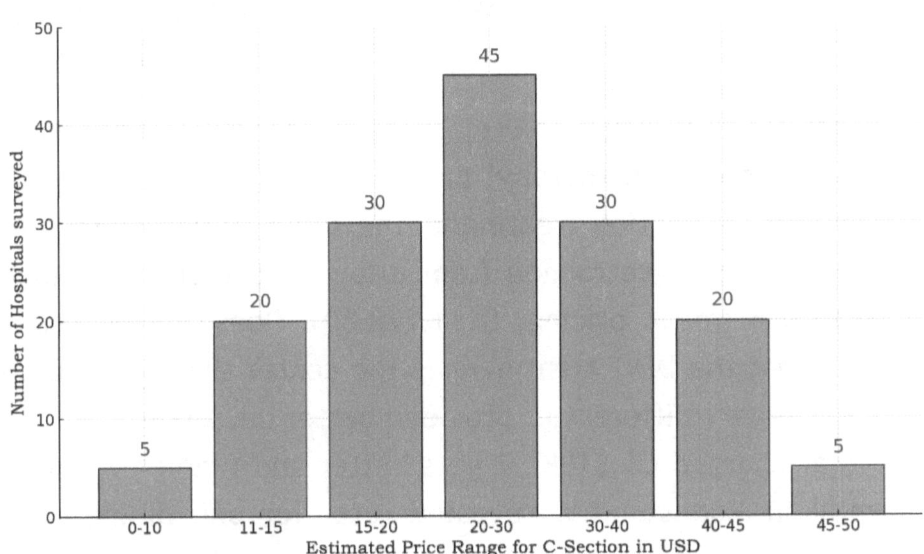

Exhibit 9.1: C-Section Pricing Variation. Numbers on top of bars are prices in US$'s. Courtesy: WSJ, Secondary research

The graph illustrates the distribution of median charges for C-sections across different hospitals. The X-axis represents the price ranges, while the vertical bars above indicate the number of hospitals falling within each price range.

As we see, we have five hospitals charging up to US $10K at the lower end and another five charging between US $45-50K for C-Sections. A 10X difference for a similar procedure!

In 2022, I was diagnosed with late-stage Colorectal Cancer. I was in India then. Everything looked nebulous. As I started looking up options for the regimen that would include radiotherapy, multiple surgeries, adjuvant chemo, etc, I was given budgets that ranged from INR 30L (~US $ 40K) to INR 150L (~US 200K). A 5X variation. Intrigued, I googled for additional studies to see if, indeed, this was the case around the world. I found this study, which was reported in WSJ[31] (Wall Street Journal). It just blows your mind.

Fifty-two hospitals were studied for IMRT (intensity-modulated radiation therapy) prices. They all listed a fee for a standard 28-fraction treatment, the same IMRT for Prostate Cancer. The charges ranged from a low of $18,368 to a high of $399,056 (mean pricing, $111,728.80). Does anyone really believe that the IMRT treatment in the center that charged US $400K was very different or provided better outcomes from the one that charged US $18K? It gets better and funnier. A Sutter hospital in Modesto, Ca, revealed rates for one billing code representing complex cardiac procedures in fragile patients that varied from $89,752 to $515,697, depending on the insurance plan. Mind Bending, to say the least.

Numerous studies have found that quality or outcome is no better or worse at high-price hospitals. "We have not found evidence that price is a great signal for quality," said Michael Chernew, the Leonard D. Schaeffer Professor of Health Care Policy at Harvard Medical School[32]. The Journal of Economics published a study that states that for consumers, the prices paid for surgery at some hospitals in the U.S. were more than double the prices at others. This is according to an analysis of 88 million privately insured citizens.

---

[31] Lagnado, L. (2010, December 7). A device to kill cancer, lift revenue. The Wall Street Journal
[32] Chernew, M. E., Dafny, L. S., & Pany, M. J. (2020, March 10). A proposal to cap provider prices and price growth in the commercial health-care market. Brookings Institution.

Another study[33] looked at the profits of more than 2,800 hospitals over a decade and found hospitals that boosted margins didn't cut costs but instead raised revenue by increasing the rates they charged to insurers. Cutting costs is hard work. Hospitals are just plain lazy. Keep bumping up prices...easy-peasy.

In most other purchases, whether consumable items or services, we are accustomed to seeing or experiencing a clear improvement in quality for the premium we pay. However, this expectation does not hold true in healthcare.

Understanding hospital pricing is a challenge—even for doctors. Let alone patients and general citizens. The discrepancies in costs and charges often defy logic, leading to the following conclusive observations:

1. Hospital pricing often bears little relation to actual costs.

2. There is no consistent connection between pricing and quality or patient outcomes.

3. High-end, fancy hospitals do not guarantee better medical results.

4. Hospital pricing operates in a chaotic, almost arbitrary manner—a "La La Land" of unpredictability.

Given that hospital pricing is opaque and veiled in secrecy and chaos, this is an area that will see a lot of innovation and disruption. The megatrends are clear, and the writing is on the wall. Price transparency in hospital services is a matter of WHEN

---

[33] Ly, D. P., & Cutler, D. M. (2018). Factors of U.S. hospitals associated with improved profit margins: An observational study. Journal of General Internal Medicine, 33(7), 1020–1027.

and not IF. Hospital services will become more "shoppable" once there is a level of sanity and transparency in pricing. Patients must be provided the ability to shop for healthcare. We will turn to this in the next chapter.

In the meanwhile, may I request you to ponder over the questions below as we get to the end of this chapter:

1. Do you think that Hospital Pricing is Arbitrary?

2. Do patients generally feel that hospital fees are complicated, opaque, and stressful?

3. Is there a massive difference between the list price and the price negotiated with insurance?

4. Should we force hospitals to publish pricing and make it more transparent?

5. Is it wrong for hospitals to have discriminatory pricing for different population segments?

6. Who will prevail in the battle of pricing between hospitals and insurance?

I would be keen to hear your views. Let us now examine how shoppable healthcare is. Up next.

Chapter 10

Healthcare Shopping

"Imagine booking a flight without knowing the price until after you land. That's healthcare."

We are used to shopping for airline tickets, car rentals, and other services. This is possible because there is a level of price transparency, and the final costs don't change at the end of the consumption or service experience. In healthcare, where there seems to be no method to pricing, price transparency is, at best, a nebulous concept. The idea to ponder is whether price transparency is ever possible in healthcare. Is it practical? Would hospitals play ball?

Before continuing, I would like my doctor reader to ponder the questions below.

1. Do you discuss the cost of care with your patients?

2. Do you have access to an accurate cost estimate of the care you have planned for your patient?

3. Do you wonder about the basis and rationale of frequent price increases?

4. Do you think price transparency is important?

Answers to the above might give us clues to resolving the Price Transparency Conundrum in hospitals.

Price transparency for healthcare procedures means allowing individuals to "shop around," just as one would before buying any expensive item, such as a car or an airline ticket. Can pricing, outcomes, demographics, and co-morbidities be adequately simplified and factored in to ensure that comparisons are meaningful?

I have absolutely no doubts in my mind that healthcare should be and can be made shoppable. Hospital management will obviously resist. They will find reasons to avoid publishing or promoting pricing transparency. The excuses will be around complexity, co-morbidities, etc., and the idea that healthcare, unlike aviation, hotels, and car rentals, is not shoppable. Some of this is valid. However, there are several hundreds of procedures and medical service categories that are either undifferentiated, predictable, or standard. It must theoretically be possible to at least receive credible pricing details for such services. Even this is unavailable. Remember the irrational pricing examples I narrated in the earlier chapter surrounding IMRT and C-Sections? I don't trust that private hospitals will give me pricing that is reasonable, fair, and accurate. Looks like I am not alone.

See Exhibit 10.1 below. There is a huge trust deficit when it comes to hospital pricing. People trust the payer or insurance company more than they would the provider, as per the McKinsey survey below. Especially when it comes to information surrounding costs of a procedure/medical service.

TRUST DEFICIT WITH HOSPITALS?

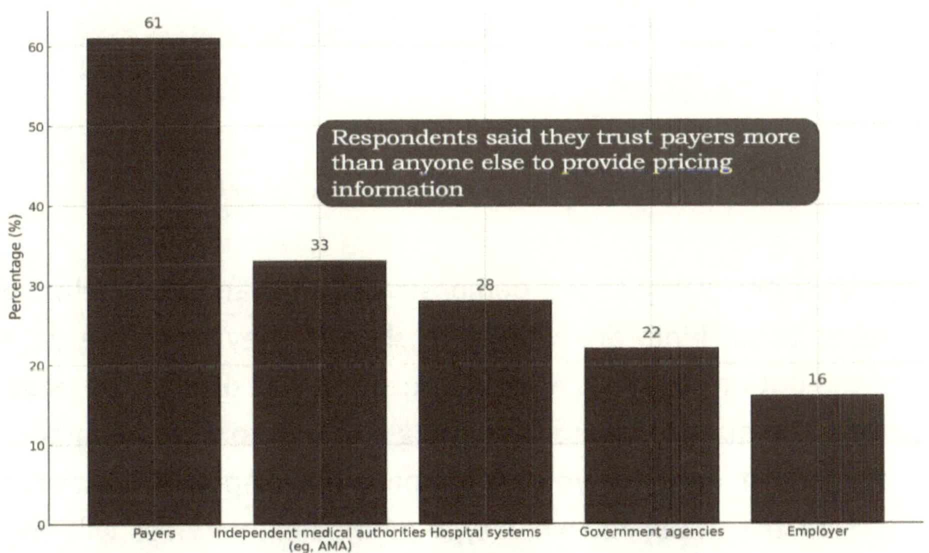

Exhibit 10.1: Price Transparency Conundrum. Courtesy: McKinsey & Company Analysis

This leads us to the natural question. Is there indeed demand for "shopping" in healthcare? Based on Exhibit 10.1, if we were to offer competitive pricing across clinics and hospitals, would people shop for healthcare? An "uberization" of sorts in healthcare.

Exhibit 10.2 provides an unambiguous answer. A resounding YES!

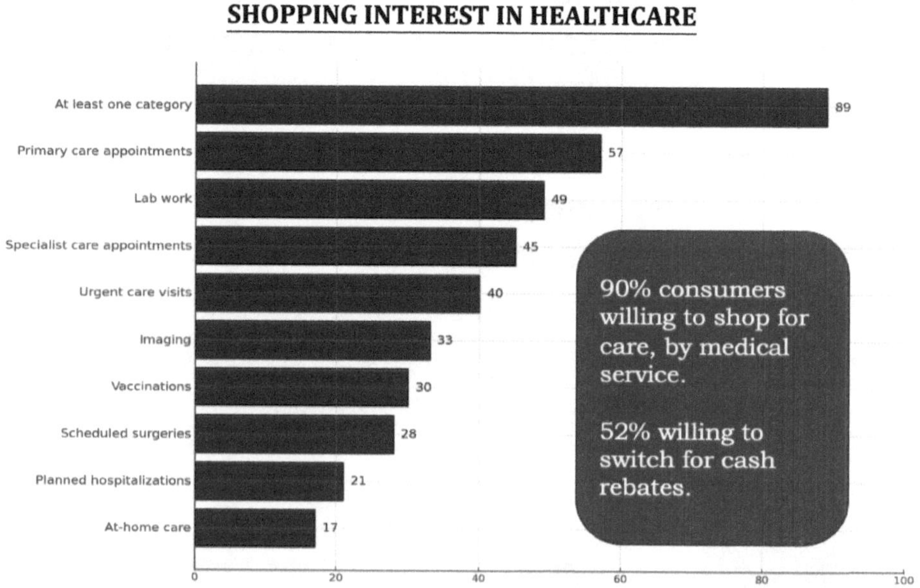

SHOPPING INTEREST IN HEALTHCARE

Exhibit 10.2: Healthcare Shopping. Courtesy: McKinsey & Company Analysis

The McKinsey study above demonstrates that an overwhelming number of patients are willing to shop if they have the data and the option to do so. A simple question was part of the large survey. The question was: "Assuming a search tool was available that made it easy for you to compare out-of-pocket costs for different hospitals, for what type of medical services will you use such a tool?" The graph summarizes the result. Almost

90% said they would shop. Even if it is for just one category of medical service.

To quote McKinsey, "Affordability is a top concern. Almost 90% percent express interest in shopping for at least one category of care, and if given the option, up to 52 percent of consumers are willing to switch providers (for example, choosing a different physician or health system) in return for cash rebates". This establishes that people want to shop for healthcare. We also know that most people don't trust hospitals with pricing.

But is healthcare shoppable? Absolutely YES. Says another McKinsey analysis. See Exhibit 10.3.

IS HEALTHCARE SHOPPABLE?

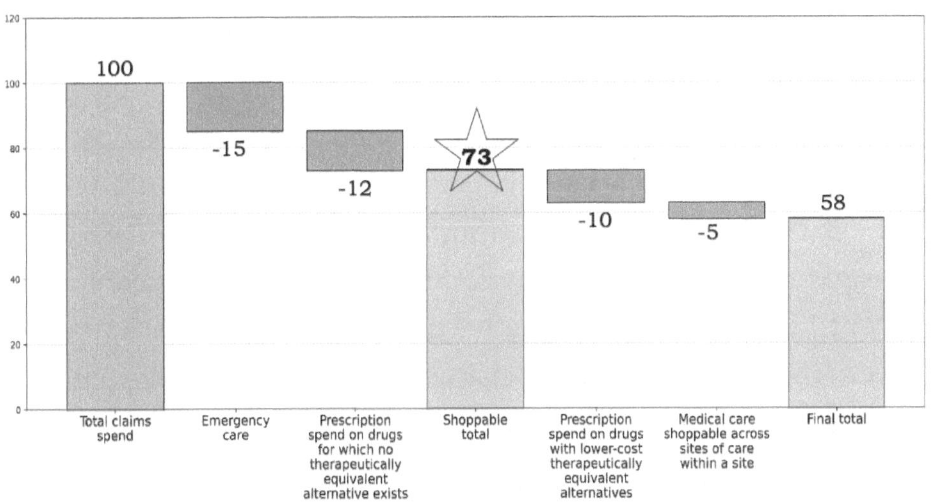

Exhibit 10.3: 73% of commercial claims in US are shoppable. Courtesy: McKinsey & Company Analysis

According to this McKinsey study, 73% of US commercial claims are shoppable. Commercial claims account for much of hospital profits in the United States. Promoting healthcare shopping would have substantial implications for hospitals across the spectrum. But hospitals will resist it tooth and nail. They have grown mostly on the back of raising rates and prices. Mostly surreptitiously. It is like asking a lazy, spoilt child to start working hard again on the subjects he hates the most, like math or physics. Unlikely to happen based on historical behavioral patterns. Hospitals in the US didn't seem to care even about a Federal Act that mandated Pricing Transparency. In the year 2021, an unprecedented rule was made effective in the US. It was called: "The Hospital Price Transparency Final Rule[34]".

The rule required hospitals to post payer-specific negotiated prices, discounted cash prices, and standard charges for all items and services in a machine-readable format. The rule also mandated a customer-friendly list of such price-related information for 300 shoppable services, of which 70 services were specified in the rule, and the remaining 230 were left to the choice of the hospital. The govt mandate also included a penalty ranging from $300 to up to $5500 per day for hospitals based on size for non-compliance. The goal of the rule was to rein in costs and promote transparency. The rule uses price transparency intending to reduce information asymmetry, permit benchmarking among hospitals, and allow patients and payers to make informed decisions. Benefits from transparency could percolate and help reduce healthcare costs.

Despite all these measures, compliance remains low. Several years down the line, the rule seems to have had little impact, as evidenced by large price variations between hospitals that still seem widespread without adequate basis. This in a mature

---

[34] Centers for Medicare & Medicaid Services. (2021). Hospital price transparency overview. U.S. Department of Health & Human Services.

market like the US where insurance companies also wield enormous bargaining power. One can imagine the situation in less mature and other emerging economies.

I'm sure governments around the world are looking at this closely. Hospitals for a while have been behaving like rebellious, spoilt teenage brats when it comes to Pricing. But this change is required for their own good. Pricing Transparency will force hospitals that charge premium rates for undifferentiated services to redefine their value propositions or prepare for compromise on margins. At the same time, high-performing hospitals whose rates do not reflect their value, and quality will be better equipped to engage payers and patients with data substantiating that their current rates need to align with their true value. Price transparency rules and pricing innovations can truly change the healthcare landscape in very profound ways as policies, economics, and medical science converge and mature.

It is a good thing, and Adam Smith would be delighted. Hospital administrators, not so much, I guess. On Pricing, hospitals are getting away with murder!

The Big Fight: Hospitals v/s Insurance Companies

There is a growing trust deficit among citizens regarding hospitals, particularly concerning the transparency of pricing information. This seems to be extending to other players in the ecosystem including governments, regulators, etc. I sense an opportunity for insurance companies. If they are sensitive and alert to the situation, they could seize the opportunity and dramatically change the landscape.

Insurers could invest heavily in consumer-facing technology. Empower the widespread adoption of healthcare shopping platforms. Encourage hospitals that are willing to publish and promote pricing transparency instead of the ones that like to keep it arcane and mysterious. Insurance companies could lobby with governments and regulators to enhance the power of the federal mandates to improve compliance amongst hospitals. This could unleash a new wave of innovation, and the impact of this will be profound. This leads us to a natural question?

Hospitals v/s Insurers. Who will win this fight, and Who is right?

This is a difficult question to answer unambiguously. Firstly, insurers and healthcare providers must remind themselves that they have a shared interest in making sure that medical treatment is better coordinated. This reduces costs for hospitals and reins in premiums for insurers. Chronic Inflation, constant clinical labor shortages, and other challenging macroeconomic conditions could propel further increases in healthcare costs over the next few years. This could lead to higher out-of-pocket costs and/or higher insurance premiums for patients. Hospital Pricing will be an area of focus for politicians and economists in the years to come. And hospitals must become more flexible and willing to look closely at efficiencies to reduce the overall burden of healthcare costs. Price transparency will resolve the asymmetry in rate information by requiring payers and hospitals to publish rates and requiring payers to provide portals that patients can access to estimate out-of-pocket expenses. Also, the ability to choose or switch between providers and clinics. If I were to pick sides, assuming nothing changes with hospital behavior on pricing, my bet would be on the Insurers. Because, as the market matures and insurance penetration increases, they can control both patient flow and payments.

Doctors cannot remain isolated from these crucial matters. Their active influence is crucial in determining how pricing policy unfolds and gets implemented. This leads me to wonder: are there ways we can tweak our payment models to hospitals and doctors that might change the way hospitals behave? Let us look at the payment models that are in vogue and newer payment models, also called APM's (alternate payment models) that are emerging. Up Next.

Chapter 11

Payment Models in Healthcare

"Incentives drive behavior. And right now, the incentive in healthcare is to do more, not better."

Hospital Payments

Historically, and even as I write this, FFS or fee-for-service has been and continues to be the most dominant payment method. Hospitals are paid for each service or episode of care in this payment system. In an FFS payment model, all the risk is with the Patient and/or the Payer. Hospitals get paid for doing stuff, and there is little accountability for value or results. Doctors and hospitals can get away with poor care coordination and even poorer alignment. Results generally don't matter. In the event of a poor outcome, they can counsel, then shrug, then say, "We did our best," and by the way, "Please pay on the way out". Hospitals and Doctors have little to no risk in an FFS model. Hence, there is no incentive to move away from the current model. I am probably exaggerating to make a point. Undoubtedly, hospitals and doctors care about their reputations and would mostly do the right thing. But by its very nature the FFS model doesn't hold hospitals and/or doctors directly accountable for outcomes.

Payment models also have a direct implication on the level and proportion of diagnosis and treatment that patients receive. The FFS model poses clear risks of over-treatment and over-diagnosis. The FFS system favors hospitals and doctors financially whilst assuming almost zero risk for outcomes.

This situation may not be tenable in the long run, especially as bargaining power shifts away from doctors and hospitals to insurers, regulators, and healthcare consumers (a.k.a. patients). Hospitals are currently both financially designed and incentivized to make money by caring for sick people. Keeping populations healthy may well put them out of business. It seems perverse but is the truth.

Research scholars, health authorities and patient action groups have been debating payment reforms (especially in the US) for a while. A model that best achieves cost savings and assures the best levels of care and outcomes for patients. Advances in healthcare financing and, more importantly, the debate on value in healthcare has resulted in the development and deployment of several new payment models. These new-age payment models are often referred to as APMs or Alternate Payment Models.

Let us examine the payment model landscape and then discuss the practical implications of APMs as the chorus for the shift towards value-based care from sheer volume-based atrocity finds more resonance.

There are probably six broad payment models that can be seen in circulation. These are briefly outlined and defined below:

1. **<u>Fee for Service (FFS) Payment</u>**

   Payment for each service and unit of care. Based on individual encounters. (the most common mode).

2. **<u>Bundled Payment (Episode Based)</u>**

   The sum of Individual Units of Care. The focus is on an entire episode of care instead of isolated encounters. (gaining traction as VBC or value-based care becomes more popular).

3. **Pay for Performance or Value-Based Care (VBC)**

   Payments are made to healthcare providers based on meeting predetermined performance thresholds that are quantifiable and measurable. This system is still in its infancy but slowly gaining some ground. (unpredictability and non-linearity of individual biological response to treatment make measurement challenging).

4. **Capitation (per capita)**

   A payment method where providers receive a fixed amount of money before service delivery to provide agreed-upon services for each registered individual over a fixed period. A model that encourages hospitals to keep their populations healthy and out of hospitals. Seems like a nice idea but has its shares of cons. Like limiting services within the payment level approved, thus compromising on quality of care.

5. **Case-Based/Diagnosis Related Groups (DRG) Payments**

   Providers are paid a fixed amount per case for each diagnosis, admission, or discharge.

6. **Accountable Care Organizations - ACO**

   Several Care Groups align together under a common umbrella to provide high-quality care.

Essentially, all payment models except FFS are attempts towards some form and shape of VBC (value-based care). All the APMs, as listed above, structure provider payment to better incentivize high-quality and cost-efficient care. Ofcourse, none of them are flawless.

Exhibits 11.1 and 11.2 capture the pros and cons of an FFS and VBC-based payment system. The summary is not exhaustive.

Only to serve the purpose of a discussion to move away from FFS to more performance-based payment systems.

FEE FOR SERVICE PAYMENT CHARACTERISTICS

Fee-for-service	
Characteristic	
• Payment for each unit of care	
Pros	**Cons**
• Well-established fee schedules	• High financial cost to the system
• Fewer restrictions on the quantity of patient visits	• Minimal financial risk for providers
	• Low incentives for quality
	• Low incentives for efficiency
	• Minimal incentives for care coordination
	• Increase in volume of unnecessary care

Exhibit 11.1: FFS Pros and Cons
Source: Economist Impact

VALUE-BASED CARE (VBC) PAYMENT CHARACTERISTICS

Pay for performance (value-based payments/purchasing)	
Characteristic	
• An attached financial incentive or disincentive to a payment model based on a provider's performance	
Example	
• Hospital Readmissions Reduction Program	
Pros	**Cons**
• Greater focus on quality over quantity	• Administrative complexity
• More transparency	• May not reflect community need
• No need to alter payment model structure	• Limited impact on patient outcomes
• Develops strategic targets	• Challenges with socioeconomically disadvantaged populations
• Greater visibility offered by micro-level data	• Data lag
	• Delayed payments
	• Gaming the system through cherry-picking and other methods

Exhibit 11.2: VBC or Pay for Performance (P4P) Pros and Cons
Source: Economist Impact

Despite the growing chorus for VBC APMs, the adoption has been rather slow and hesitant. There is no incentive for hospitals to make the shift on their own. Even in the US, all care is predominantly FFS, as is clear in Exhibit 11.3. The trend is slowly increasing but the rate of change towards VBC and away from FFS still is abysmally low, in my opinion.

MAJORITY OF HEALTH SYSTEMS REVENUE REMAINS FFS

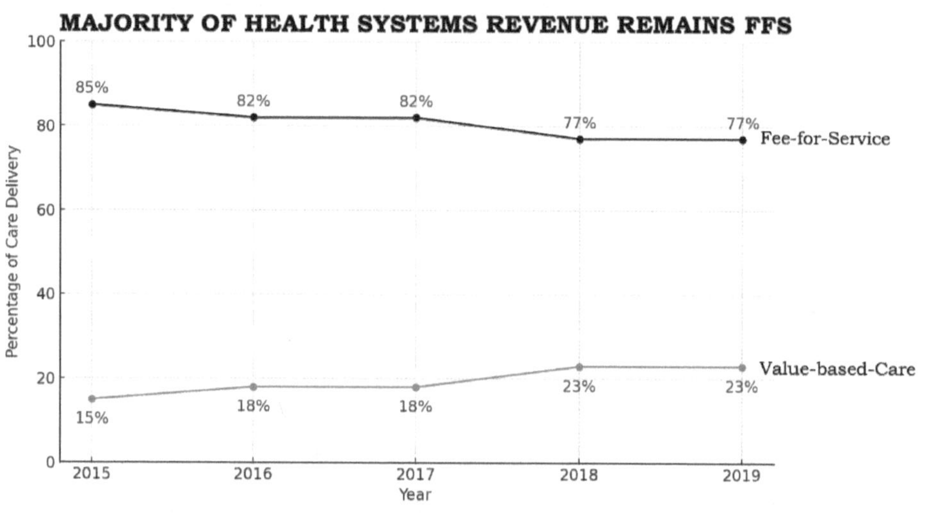

Exhibit 11.3: Adoption of APMs. Courtesy: The Academy Research Strategic Tracking Survey 2019

FFS still contributes to around 70-80% of all care in the US. Only large integrated hospital systems that have their health insurance plans seem to be able to or even motivated to adopt VBC or another form of APM. Even though the pace has been slow, there is some hope. We must examine the forces that can help propel this transition.

Exhibit 11.4 captures the enablers that drive the transition to VBC payment models.

VALUE-BASED PAYMENT MODEL ENABLERS

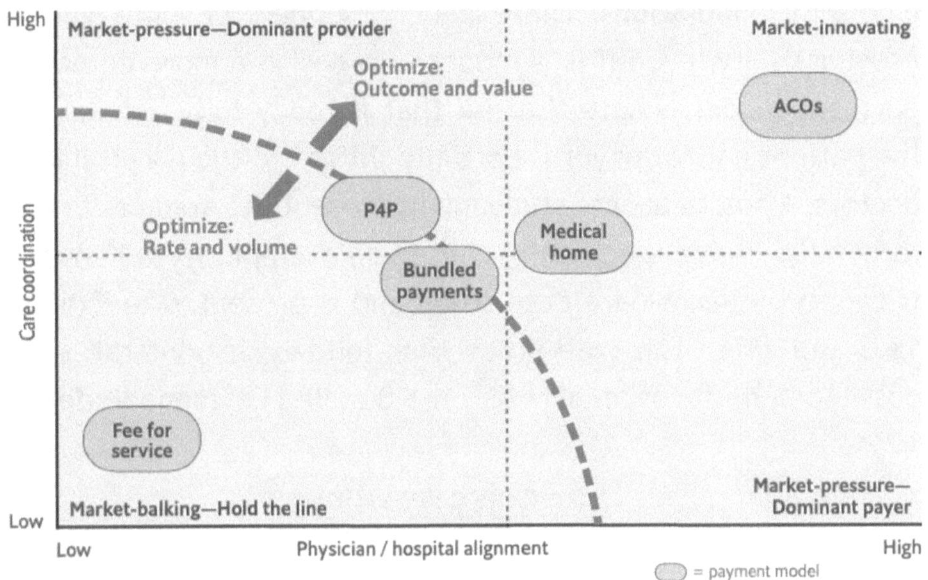

Exhibit 11.4: Forces shaping Payment Models
Source: American College of Cardiology, Larry Sobal, The Transition to Value, 2018
Graphic insight: Economist Impact, adapted from source listed above.

The graphic provides a compelling picture. The contrast is clear. The X-axis is a measure of the level of alignment between hospitals and physicians. The Y-axis is a measure of the levels of care coordination. We know that these measures are poor today in most hospitals worldwide. Hence FFS thrives.

FFS can flourish when the physician-hospital alignment and care coordination are both low/poor. It grows on the back of optimizing volumes and rates charged. APM, on the other hand, requires better alignment and coordination, a feature that is rare in most hospitals today. These models accentuate the need to optimize value and outcomes. Value-Based Care APMs force us to understand factors that impact value, costs, and outcomes. It is hard work, but hospitals and doctors owe it to their populations. There is a crying need for some level of accountability, even if it is modest. To design a more equitable payment model, where the risk that is today fully assumed by the patient and/or payer is partially shifted to the hospitals and doctors. A practical case study might present the argument more forcefully. I have specifically chosen an example from Kenya. It is called the Mom-Care case study and is presented in Exhibits 11.5 and 11.6. The case study that follows demonstrates the possible benefits of an APM like the Bundled Payment Model.

MOM CARE CASE-STUDY

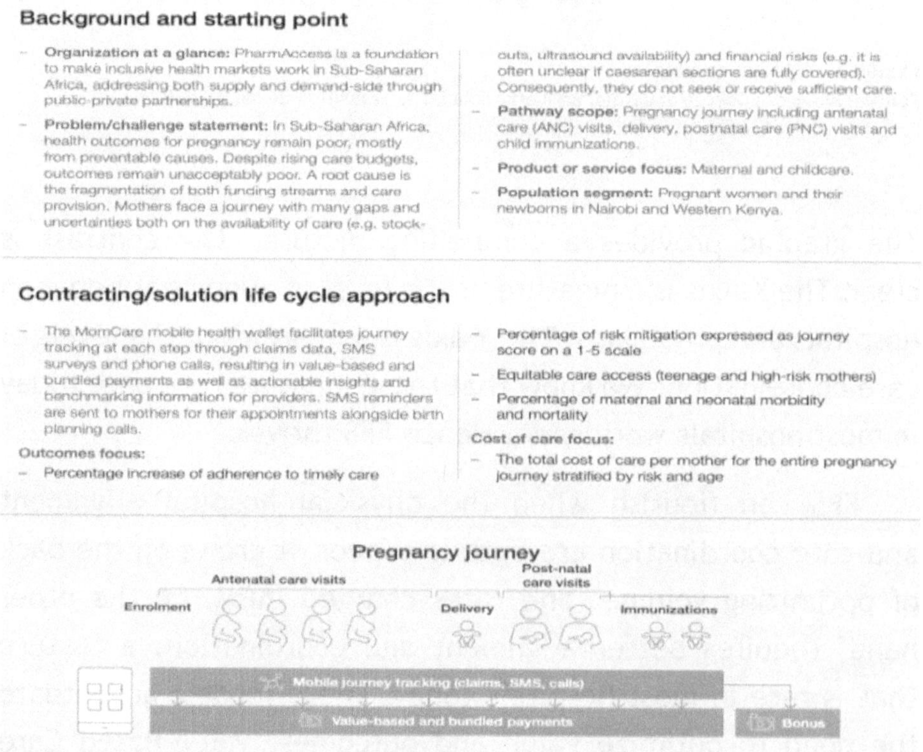
Background and starting point
– Organization at a glance: PharmAccess is a foundation to make inclusive health markets work in Sub-Saharan Africa, addressing both supply and demand-side through public-private partnerships.
– Problem/challenge statement: In Sub-Saharan Africa, health outcomes for pregnancy remain poor, mostly from preventable causes. Despite rising care budgets, outcomes remain unacceptably poor. A root cause is the fragmentation of both funding streams and care provision. Mothers face a journey with many gaps and uncertainties both on the availability of care (e.g. stock-outs, ultrasound availability) and financial risks (e.g. it is often unclear if caesarean sections are fully covered). Consequently, they do not seek or receive sufficient care.
– Pathway scope: Pregnancy journey including antenatal care (ANC) visits, delivery, postnatal care (PNC) visits and child immunizations.
– Product or service focus: Maternal and childcare.
– Population segment: Pregnant women and their newborns in Nairobi and Western Kenya.
Contracting/solution life cycle approach
– The MomCare mobile health wallet facilitates journey tracking at each step through claims data, SMS surveys and phone calls, resulting in value-based and bundled payments as well as actionable insights and benchmarking information for providers. SMS reminders are sent to mothers for their appointments alongside birth planning calls.
Outcomes focus:
– Percentage increase of adherence to timely care
– Percentage of risk mitigation expressed as journey score on a 1-5 scale
– Equitable care access (teenage and high-risk mothers)
– Percentage of maternal and neonatal morbidity and mortality
Cost of care focus:
– The total cost of care per mother for the entire pregnancy journey stratified by risk and age
Pregnancy journey
Antenatal care visits
Post-natal care visits
Enrolment
Delivery
Immunizations
Mobile journey tracking (claims, SMS, calls)
Value-based and bundled payments
Bonus

Exhibit 11.5: Improving maternal and neonatal outcomes in Africa.
Courtesy: PharmAccess Foundation. Graphics: Adapted from Economist Impact

That health outcomes remain poor for pregnant women in sub-Saharan Africa is a widely known fact. This despite much of the poor outcomes are easily preventable. Government interventions, and increased care budgets didn't improve the outcome metrics. PharmAccess (a foundation that addresses healthcare gaps in Africa) attempted a Bundled Pay Model for Pregnancy that included the spectrum (entire episode) from ante-natal care to delivery to post-natal evaluations and immunizations. The enrolments also included up to 10% of very high-risk pregnancies. The study covered over 29,000 mothers in Kenya (mostly in Nairobi and rural areas)

MOM CARE CASE-STUDY

Accessibility and Affordability

1. Over 29,000 mothers in Kenya were given access to pregnancy care, including ~10% of high-risk mothers.
2. Mothers empowered through increased awareness about delivery signs, perinatal danger signs, breastfeeding and appointment reminders.
3. Early risk stratification improved care for high-risk mothers.

Quantitative (Clinical and Economic)

1. 16% increase in adherence to antenatal care visits for all mothers and a 25% increase for high-risk mothers.
2. 15% increase in antenatal care visits that have a full set of haemoglobin, syphilis, HIV, blood glucose, urine, and tuberculosis tests.
3. 17% increase in completed pregnancy journeys (≥3 out of 5).
4. 37% decrease in journey costs for women who deliver through caesarean section.

Exhibit 11.6: Bundled Payment Model Impact on Outcomes. Courtesy: PharmAccess Foundation

The results are astounding. Studies showed a 16% increase in adherence to ante-natal visits. For high-risk, it had risen by 25%. There was almost a 20% increase in completed pregnancy journeys, with a corresponding dip of almost 40% in overall costs. I feel like bowing down and saluting the women folk (Asante Sana Mama) who participated in this study. They gave themselves and their unborn babies better odds in resource-constrained situations. If poorly resourced areas like sub-Saharan Africa, where women folk face challenges we probably cannot even imagine, can lead the way and demonstrate these results, surely, we have no reason or excuse not to investigate and invest more in similar APM's around the world.

Let us now look at how doctors are compensated and the various Physician Payment models in vogue. Physicians and Hospital administration may not be aligned in general, but when it comes to payment models, I suspect they may be "hand-in-glove".

Physician Payments

The physician compensation model evolves with the progression of their careers. Most start with a simple straight salary model to a more production and incentive-based model as their career matures and they have established their reputation and practice. It seems similar to the ways artists' and athletes' compensations evolve over their careers.

In this section, I wanted to focus mainly on the non-cash side of what is important to doctors. Most hospital and doctor negotiations around compensation are largely monetary. However, we took a peek into the minds and psyche of our doctors in Chapter 2. Monies are undoubtedly important, but hospital managements are doing a very poor job in trying to make our doctors' lives easier. And it is not always about money.

Before I get to that, let me outline the main payment models that are in vogue.

Six compensation model variations seem to be prevalent today. This is not exhaustive. Newer models may evolve as hospital payments come under pressure to shift from volume to value.

1. **Salary (plus Bonus)**: Physicians receive a flat salary for performing their job responsibilities. This is a consistent wage that is unrelated to performance, productivity, or other variables. Generally, younger physicians prefer a straight salary as it offers security. However, there is no incentive to advance skills or participate in larger organizational efforts to grow the practice. Straight salary works best in ensuring patients receive the most optimum and appropriate care. Additional bonuses linked to some performance or quality measures could be added to promote broader organizational participation. This model is essentially worry-free for young physicians but could stymie entrepreneurship or support minimum-effort work standards.

2. **Minimum Income Guarantee**: Akin to a straight salary, in this model, the employer agrees to provide income support to the physician for a specific period. The guaranteed amount is not dependent upon volume, productivity, or performance. The income generated by the physician is set off against the minimum guaranteed amount. Once the physician starts earning over the threshold, compensation is generally given as a percentage for the additional amounts. This model offers security and incentivizes the physician to cross the threshold and generate more. However, good performance and quality of care could be compromised.

3. **Fee For Service (FFS):** This model rewards highly productive physicians and offers motivation to increase patient loads. It allows productive doctors to reap the rewards of their hard work and protects them from negative financial consequences when team members are not as productive. However, it may foster unhealthy competition as doctors may compete for patients and could prevent the best care for the patient. Experts and critics also suggest that overdiagnosis and over-treatment are common when doctors are compensated under this model.

4. **Net Revenue:** Doctors are paid based on their revenue and less expenses. It could be on an individualized basis or at the level of the practice group. After expenses, the remaining revenues are allocated among the group's physicians based on a pre-determined and agreed-upon proportion. A potential drawback of the model is its assumption that all physicians possess equal levels of skill, productivity, and, perhaps most crucially, motivation to prioritize the group's financial interests.

5. **Performance-Based (Pay for Performance or P4P):** Specific metrics, best practices, and patient satisfaction are used to assess provider performance and ensure organizational goals are met. Value or performance-based care uses this data to regulate healthcare processes and improve the quality of patient care. Unlike other compensation models, there is a financial incentive for keeping patients healthy

with preventative care and lifestyle counseling. It shifts the focus to value over volume. The goal is to keep patients out of hospitals. However, the demands of a performance-based system can be too much for some physicians, leading to lower job satisfaction and provider burnout. Also, physicians may lose compensation if they work for an organization that lacks the staff, training, and resources to track key performance data to support true value-based care.

6. **Capitated Payment Model**: This is a payment model where physicians/providers receive a fixed fee for each patient under their care, regardless of the services rendered. Models like these, including bundled payments, are designed to enhance cost efficiency and encourage coordinated care by motivating physicians to provide high-quality care within the budgeted amount. Money is made by keeping citizens/patients healthy and out of hospitals.

Physician recruitment is a complex process[35] but a disproportionate amount of time and energy is occupied by financial considerations. Let us now spend a few minutes on ways to attract and recruit physicians with incentives that are not cash related.

---

[35] The American Medical Association (AMA) releases a series of Policy Research Perspectives that examine methods, such as salary and productivity, used to compensate physicians. Readers interested in a deep dive can visit the AMA website. It is a fascinating read.

Healthcare organizations and medical facilities need to consider several non-compensation factors to attract and retain talented physicians. Outlined below are some key non-cash portions that may seem relevant and meaningful to many physicians:

1. **Work-Life Balance**: Physicians often face demanding schedules, making it essential to create a work environment that fosters work-life balance. Offering flexible working hours, manageable call rotations, and adequate time off can attract prospective physicians. Younger physicians especially, place a high premium on this and must be considered.

2. **Quality of Life**: Factors such as the location of the facility, proximity to family and friends, cost of living, recreational opportunities, and overall community atmosphere can significantly impact a physician's quality of life.

3. **Career Development and Advancement**: Physicians, like any other professionals, want opportunities for growth and career advancement. Showing a commitment to supporting their professional development through continuing medical education, mentorship programs, research opportunities, and leadership roles can attract talented physicians. One idea is to provide a 5-year career progression plan based on specific criteria. People want security and growth.

4. **Collaborative and Supportive Team**: Physicians appreciate a collaborative and supportive work

environment. A culture that fosters teamwork, open communication, and camaraderie can be key to attracting and retaining them. Additionally, the opportunity to work in a multi-specialty group, which enhances collaboration and continuity of care, can be particularly appealing.

5. **Technology and Facilities:** Modern medical facilities and access to cutting-edge technology are crucial for physicians dedicated to delivering high-quality patient care. Showing a commitment to investing in advanced equipment and infrastructure can be a strong incentive for attracting prospective candidates.

6. **Reputation and Patient Population:** A healthcare organization's reputation, patient population, and case complexity can influence a physician's decision to join. A facility known for excellence in patient care and positive patient outcomes will attract physicians seeking to make a meaningful impact.

7. **Administrative Support:** Physicians want to focus on patient care rather than administrative and billing tasks. A strong administrative support system, including assistance with paperwork, billing, and other non-clinical tasks, can make a medical practice more appealing.

8. **Malpractice Insurance and Benefits:** Providing comprehensive malpractice insurance coverage and attractive benefits packages can be essential factors in attracting physicians.

9. **Research and Academic Opportunities:** Many physicians are interested in research or academic duties, access to research or grant funding, collaborations with academic institutions, and opportunities to teach can be decisive factors.

10. **Leadership Opportunities:** Demonstrating a commitment to involving physicians in decision-making processes and providing opportunities for leadership roles within the organization can be attractive to those seeking to have a greater impact on healthcare delivery.

Finally, many physicians weigh the advantages and disadvantages of being employed versus practicing independently[36]. Private hospital owners, I have met, tend to prefer having doctors (especially seniors) on a pure fee-for-service model without any base or fixed salary commitment. However, the situation remains unclear as to which model works best. I guess, it depends on the individual and the context. Exhibit 11.7 below, provides a comparative analysis based on an informal survey of hospitals and physicians. This is not a scientific study, and the analysis is subjective for the most part and gleaned from interviews and informal conversations with my doctor friends.

---

[36] HeyInfluent. Employed vs private practice: Pros and cons.

COMPARATIVE ANALYSIS

EMPLOYED PHYSICAN	INDEPENDENT PRACTITIONER
Generally Steady And Secure Pay-check	Variable Pay-check But Relatively Higher Earn
Deal With Red-tape And Bureaucracy	Lot Of Autonomy
Staff Available To Handle Admin Tasks	Have To Worry About Admin Tasks Like Billing Etc
Staff To Handle Tech And Regulatory	Have To Worry About Tech And Regulatory
Environment To Interact And Learn From Peers	Less Opportunity To Engage And Learn
Predictable Work/Life Balance But Have To Squeeze Patients	Not Predictable Albeit Greater Ability To Schedule
Lesser Sense Of Urgency And Productivity	Higher Productivity And Sense Of Urgency
No Control Over Budgets And Staff	Higher Control Over Staff And Budgets
Can Sleep At Peace As Someone Managing Patients	Always At Risk If Something Happens To Patients At Night
No Control over Compensation Model	Can Design Own Compensation Model
Have Productivity Targets Imposed	Can Decide Targets And Models
Relatively Lower Morale	Higher Morale Relatively
Hospitals Tend To Lose Monies On Fully Salaried Doctors	Hospitals Tend To Make Money On Full Fee For Service Doctors

Exhibit 11.7: Indie v/s Employed Physicians

In the next chapter, we explore the idea of value in healthcare and attempt ways to make it more quantifiable and maybe even measurable. Because, what you cannot measure, you won't be able to manage. Unless value-based care frameworks evolve to become more quantifiable which in turn can be used by hospitals to claim and justify a premium, it will probably remain an academic discussion and not see widespread deployment and application.

Chapter 12

Exploring Value in Healthcare

"Medicine teaches doctors about the body, science teaches them about disease, but too often, no one teaches them about the patient." – Inspired by Voltaire

Doctors are trained to defeat mortality, morbidity and the disease conditions afflicting the patient. They design care plans that effectively focus on this goal. And thanks to God and to our doctors for keeping us alive and well. Understandably, much of the clinical outcomes in vogue focus on metrics such as Readmissions, Sentinel Events, Near Misses, preventable mortality, reporting errors, rates of complications, and the like. However, patients can behave strangely and sound even weirder. One of my close friends from my engineering college days was dying from Glioblastoma. I was with him and the family throughout the difficult journey. He was admitted to the hospital where I served as CEO, and I maintained regular communication with the surgeons and oncologists. Every time, I would go to meet him, he would complain of an irresistible urge to pee. But pee he could not. He never once spoke about the fact that he was dying and wouldn't be around in a matter of months. This phantom urge to pee though was never a matter of concern or conversation amongst the treating doctors. I was baffled and even thought that my dying friend was just being weird and probably going nuts. The doctors never once tried to address his "urge to pee" and spent a lot of time keeping him alive. Which they did. Just another 45 days though, but during which time his phantom urge to pee only got worse. I wondered if the doctors could have accepted the inevitable mortality and just focused on making the phantom urge to pee go away...maybe he would have had better conversations with his wife and three lovely children during the last days and weeks of his life. I started to think if the focus on saving lives blinds us and our doctors on what life itself means to our patients. This fact still haunts me. Maybe I could have done better.

I faced a similar situation, with my dad. And again, I failed. My dad suffered a hip fracture and underwent surgery. The surgeons seemed pleased with the procedure and declared the operation was a success. My dad, however, couldn't walk like he could before the surgery and had to use a walker or was on a wheelchair. The immobility devastated him psychologically, and everything went downhill after that. Doctors claiming success in the procedure meant little to him. He passed away within 2 years of the surgery.

It dawned on me that patients' priorities are generally not factored into outcome measurements. This doesn't mean that the current measurements are wrong. Just that successful Clinical Outcomes need not necessarily mean successful Patient Relevant Outcomes.

I remember another story. My friend's father had suffered a stroke, and the prognosis was highly guarded. He was 84. He needed an invasive brain surgery, or the other option was just palliative. The surgery also had a high risk of patient collapsing on the table. My friend wasn't sure what might be the right course of action. Just palliate and let him die peacefully? Or take chances with the surgery. Discussions with friends and family members didn't provide much clarity. Doctors were awaiting a decision. Finally, she decided to ask her dad directly. She laid out the options to him directly with the risks associated. His response was simple, "Mole', (Malayalam for daughter) if I can watch a cricket match and have pazhampuri (banana fritters, a local delicacy in Kerala) after the surgery, then I want to take my chances." She conveyed this to the surgeon. The surgeon felt that the demand sounded reasonable. They went ahead with the surgery. He enjoyed his life for about 4 years watching many entertaining games and died of natural causes. His demand was cricket and fritters. It might seem trivial, but that is all that mattered to Ganesh-*Ettan* (as he was lovingly called). Now, shouldn't that be somehow included in the value equation?

In the classic Hindi movie, "Anand", the protagonist dying of Cancer, played by Rajesh Khanna tells his friend (Dr. Bhaskar), played by Amitabh Bachchan "Zindagi Badi Honi Chahiye, Lambi Nahi!". It loosely translates to "Life should be Big, not Long!". The idea is that living life to its fullest should always trump longevity. Maybe this is what Value is to us and our patients.

This means that exploring value in healthcare, cannot be divorced from patients' expectations, which might sometimes have little to do with any of the clinical metrics that doctors measure to claim success.

Exhibit 12.1 below showcases this dichotomy very well. It contrasts the mismatch between what matters to BrCa (breast cancer) patients and what is being measured by doctors. The data is intriguing as these patients with metastatic breast cancer disease were more concerned about things like how the future will unfold, finances, nutrition, sleep disorders, pain and the rest of it. Treating doctors on the hand were focused on mortality, complications and relapse. Clearly if the patient is dead then none of the patient's desires matter. But there is a case for including items that matter and of priority to the patient into the metrics that are measured and assessed. Doctors somehow don't seem to be able to accept death. Does it feel like a failure to them? But mortality is certain, like Taxes.

This brings us to a logical question. What is Value in Healthcare?

PATIENT REQUIREMENTS V/S MEASUREMENTS MONITORED

WHAT MATTERS TO BREAST CANCER PATIENTS...

...IS INADEQUATELY REFLECTED BY TODAY'S MEASUREMENTS[1]

Criteria (%)

Criteria	%
Worrying about the future and what lies ahead	44
Feeling too tired to do what you need or want to do	39
Health insurance or money worries	38
Eating and nutrition	37
Moving around (such as walking, climbing stairs, lifting)	33
Exercising and being physically active	33
Worrying about family, children, and friends	33
Sleep problems	32
Changes and disruptions in work, school, or home life	31
Pain or physical discomfort	31

- Mortality
- Complications
- Relapse
- Patient satisfaction
- Waiting times for diagnosis and treatment
- Pre-operative diagnosis
- Tumor data
- Surgery technique

Source: *Elevating the Patient Voice: Cancer Experience Registry Index Report 2012.*
Note: This data reflects the percentage of patients with metastatic breast cancer who responded "seriously" or "very seriously."

Exhibit 12.1: Measuring "Value" – What matters to patients

Should doctors explicitly ask patients their expectations from a procedure and include that in their design of the care plan? For example, a patient might feel most anxious about her inability to move or climb stairs when the clinician is focused on keeping her alive and away from complications. Survival and mortality trump other metrics for the clinician, but the quality of life is also equally important to a patient.

Value may be defined as quality divided by costs, where quality reflects patient outcomes and costs are the total costs for providing care, whether these be costs related to an episode or a diagnosis. Measuring value means measuring outcomes important to patients and costs using time-driven activity-based costing. This isn't perfect but can provide a basis for developing a quantifiable value measurement framework.

The idea of value-based care seems elegant, noble even, but challenges remain in mathematically quantifying patient-reported outcomes. However, including or even acknowledging these metrics will probably expand the way we understand and improve the patient experience.

In his article, "What Is Value in Health Care?" Michael E. Porter[37] highlights the importance of outcomes measurement. He defines outcomes as "results of care in terms of patients' health over time." Building on this framework, ICHOM[38], a nonprofit organization, has defined outcomes as "the results people care about most when seeking treatment, including functional improvement and the ability to live normal, productive lives."

The ICOHM effort points us in an important direction. That outcome should be measured for all patients within a well-defined disease segment (such as those with coronary artery disease). Whether they are treated via a bypass or a PCI (percutaneous coronary intervention) or simply with meds is irrelevant.

Additionally, we have already seen that there can be a Himalayan difference between what doctors and hospitals measure and what patients really care about. From my personal experiences, I think that patients just want to go about being independent, symptom-free and pursuing life without being

---

[37] Porter, M. E. (2010). What is value in health care? The New England Journal of Medicine, 363(26), 2477–2481.

[38] I highly recommend googling ICOHM. It has defined and published over 12 global standards for outcomes measurement so far.

intercepted by their medical condition. Identifying and measuring the right outcomes and defining "Value" unambiguously will pave the way for a tectonic shift in the way healthcare is delivered and consumed. This is not going to be easy as value is inherently subjective. Also, these decisions will undoubtedly be influenced by changes in capital allocations, revenue models, information asymmetry, technology disruptions, and regulations.

If you have survived this far, I'm sure there is a high likelihood you will complete the journey.

Your Prescriptions follow next. Compliance recommended ☺

Section 3

Prescriptions for Doctors

Chapter 13

Prescription 1: Move the Cheese

"When a plane crashes, we investigate the system. When a patient dies, we blame the doctor."

There is nothing non-medical about a hospital. Every facet of a hospital has a bearing on patient safety and physician well-being. For example, as a doctor, did it ever occur to you that flawed capital structuring or a poorly funded working capital design by management could affect patient safety?

When there is an adverse event, how many times have you seen patients suing the CFO or the CEO? Rarely, right? When there is a sentinel event, aren't you, as the physician summoned to explain? Isn't the likelihood of you getting sued or your reputation getting tarnished far higher than that of the CEO/CFO or even the hospital?

We forget that "Shit Happens" when MANY things go wrong SIMULTANEOUSLY. But we are very good at finding "ONE" reason because it is easier to nail a scapegoat. And we are just plain lazy to investigate and examine. I have probably become cynical and think that no one gives a damn about the truth.

Let us look at what Prof. James Reason has to say about accidents. Dr. James Reason, Professor at the University of Manchester, developed the Swiss Cheese Model in the 1990s[39]. It is a simple yet fascinating model to illustrate the complexities of error prevention and risk management, especially for complex systems. It was probably developed or applied to aviation initially but has since found applications in other fields, including healthcare, manufacturing, power plants, cybersecurity, transportation, etc.

The model is named after the characteristic Swiss cheese, symbolizing the vulnerabilities that lurk in each layer. Each

---

[39] Reason, J. (1990). Human error. Cambridge University Press.

"layer" represents a defense, such as, training, policies, processes, etc, but "holes" in the layer are gaps, and when holes in different layers align, there is a high likelihood of an adverse outcome. An error or an accident pathway is created when holes or gaps align. People responsible for governance must ensure that gaps or holes are identified and plugged. They must ensure that layers overlap so that holes in other layers are covered. "Holes" can represent active failures or latent conditions that propagate harm.

Have a look at Exhibit 13.1, where the "Swiss cheese model" has been adapted for a hospital scenario:

THE HOSPITAL SWISS CHEESE

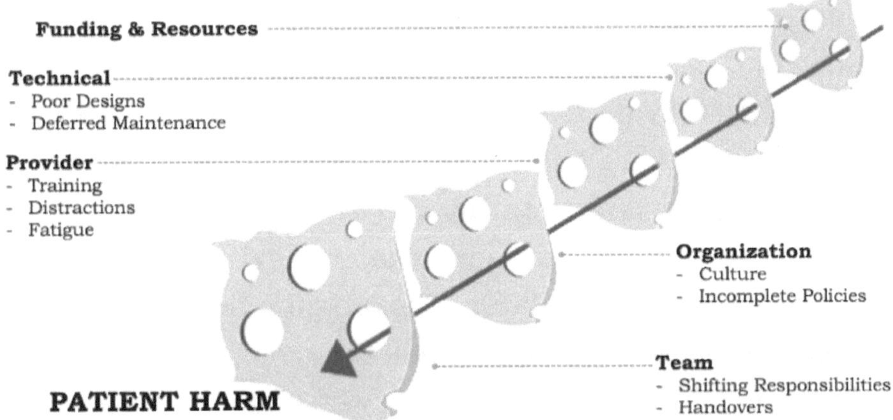

Exhibit 13.1: Accident Causation is Systemic. Courtesy: Adapted from Prof. J. Reason, JCR Post, 2000

No single layer of defense is foolproof, and the emphasis must be on multiple overlapping safeguards to prevent adverse outcomes. Accident causation is systemic, and blame cannot be entirely placed on an individual. This is the essence of the Swiss Cheese idea.

What is needed is a sincere application of resources in recognizing deficiencies in the system/processes and fixing them. Developing a risk assessment framework to assiduously identify all possible gaps in every layer of defense and constantly evolve methods to prevent harm.

However, we only respond to accidents; we never celebrate when harm is prevented or incentivize personnel whose alertness prevented a major tragedy.

Let me narrate an incident I was privy to at a large tertiary care hospital. The Neurosciences department was led by a reputed neurosurgeon. He had a high caseload and was much sought after in the region. Once he operated on a young adult, and after the regulated period in ICU, ward, and rehab, the patient was discharged. The family was thankful, and everything seemed fine. Several days later, the patient was wheeled in with complications. Symptoms and diagnostics indicated a virulent bacterial infection. Immediate intervention was needed to avoid a fatality. It was an anxious period for all concerned. The surgeon intervened, and after a revision surgery, the patient recovered. Days later, the patient's family blamed the surgeon and filed a suit against him for medical negligence and malpractice. Over-eager journalists who had no interest in the truth (not surprisingly) damaged the doctor's reputation with superficial and one-sided coverage. It was difficult to witness a conscientious, patient-centric doctor go through that ordeal. It scarred him quite deeply. Given his importance to the hospital, an investigation was ordered. The report outlined several possible causes, surgeon negligence or malpractice wasn't one of them. Some of the reasons they identified were as follows:

1. OT Maintenance: Temperature and Humidity levels weren't optimum during surgery. This could have caused bacterial colonization. Maintenance and Facility management issues?

2. Adequate funding for OT maintenance that was requested wasn't disbursed on time. Poor working capital management?

3. Possible doctor fatigue due to heavy caseload and distraction resulting in overlooking key criteria before surgery?

4. Organizational culture that possibly prevented other junior doctors or nurses from flagging any deficiency before surgery?

Several layers were breached, but it was the surgeon who was crucified. There wasn't even as much of a whisper about facility maintenance, working capital deficiency, poor culture and policies, etc, as possible reasons for the incident.

This incident made me wonder: Shouldn't hospital boards, management, and CEO also be held legally/financially/personally responsible and accountable for such adverse events? It is unlikely that this will ever happen. As a society, we tend only to see and understand proximate causes. Depth generally doesn't seem to be a hallmark of our species.

The Hospital Swiss Cheese model depicted in Exhibit 13.1 highlights some of the "holes" as listed below. You can see how something as seemingly innocuous as working capital could cause patient harm.

1. Improper and poorly designed Economics and Capital Structures with inadequate working capital can cause patient harm.

2. Poorly designed OTs, wards, nursing stations, and ICUs can cause patient harm. Compounded by irregular maintenance and calibration.

3. Lack of ongoing training for nurses, paramedics, and support staff. Poor recruitment and induction policies and poorly staffed hospitals with badly designed nurse-to-bed ratios can cause harm.

4. Fatigue and stress of care providers can cause patient harm.

5. Management and Leadership are singularly responsible for culture and policies. A culture that doesn't put safety front and center can cause serious patient harm.

6. Poorly done job goals and shoddy handovers during shift changes can cause patient harm.

When something goes wrong, we always ask, "Who was the admitting doctor?" We want quick answers. Little do we realize that asking the right questions is far more important. Wrong questions are unlikely to get the right answers. Onto Prescription No. 2 next.

Chapter 14

Prescription 2: Rx for Relax

(Maximize Vacation Time)
"Success at work means nothing if you fail at home."

What does maximizing vacation time with family have to do with economics?

The choices you make around allocating your time, energy, and talent ultimately determine your overall life experience. A bunch of "businesses" compete for your limited time, attention, and resources: trying to have a rewarding relationship with your spouse, raising great kids, contributing to the community, succeeding in your career, and so on. The problems we face in life institutions, like marriage, are not dissimilar to those of organizations. There is just a limited amount of time, energy, and talent. How much should you devote to each of these pursuits? It is an optimization problem.

Allocation of time and energy to these choices can make your life turn out to be very different from what you intended. If your resources investment strategy is unwise, the outcome can be pretty bad.

People who have a high need for achievement—and that includes many of the doctors, will tend to unconsciously allocate their time and resources to activities that yield the most tangible results. The designations we hold, the bank balance/net worth, and external paraphernalia offer the most concrete evidence to ourselves and society that we have been moving upwards and forward.

In contrast, investing time and energy in the relationship with our spouse and children typically doesn't offer that same immediate sense of visible achievement. Kids misbehave, and as teenagers, they rebel. It can be frustratingly harrowing. It took my wife and me 22 to 25 years, when we could put our hands on our hips and say, "Maybe, we raised a good kid." Also, some marriages take a long time to mature and find a place of real acceptance.

You can neglect your relationship with your spouse on a day-to-day basis. You can postpone tutoring your child or miss some of her dance lessons. Nothing happens, or so it seems. It all seems fine—until it's not. One final straw snaps the camel's back, and everything comes crashing down in a sudden, precipitous collapse.

Doctors who are driven to excel, tend to unconsciously underinvest in their families and overinvest in their careers. Intimate and loving relationships with families are the most powerful and enduring source of happiness. This means the optimum allocation of the most important resource available to us - our time. Your crowded schedules during the regular working days might make this difficult. Ergo, the recommendation is to maximize vacations. Maybe smaller duration breaks, but make it more frequent. Spending quality time with our loved ones has an enormously salutary effect on our productivity, efficiency, and outcomes at work. Also, on our mental well-being and consequently on our financials and economics.

Several studies in the US seem to indicate that families that regularly spend quality time are more likely to have better emergency savings. Children growing up in families where quality time is spent together are highly likely to graduate and also have above-average financial literacy as they grow up[40]. Correlations don't imply causation, and these studies might

---

[40] Investopedia. How to talk to kids about money—and why you should do so early.

have their flaws and limitations. But the temptation to over-invest in things that provide immediate results and under-invest in families doesn't seem like a wise investment idea overall.

Investigations into the causes of business disasters, repeatedly reveal the founder's propensity towards investing in endeavors that offered immediate gratification. Everything takes time. Not giving things time to "cook and bake" is probably one of the biggest risks we take.

The truth is, even success in our careers takes time. Everything takes longer than it should, this is the sobering truth of life. We must allow and budget for this.

The best contemporary example we can take inspiration from is none other than Jeff Bezos, who built Amazon. Bezos famously said that his "overnight success took over 10 years[41]". It took a decade of relentless effort, experimentation, and perseverance to achieve a vision with a longer-term focus than others. Founded in 1994 as a mere online bookstore during the incipient stages of internet commerce, over decades, Amazon has grown into a behemoth and shows no signs of slowing down. It took time and relentless enthusiasm, especially during the darkest of hours. Bezos has consistently emphasized the value of patience and persistence in business, advising entrepreneurs to focus on long-term goals rather than seeking immediate gratification. When seen from this perspective, personal lives reveal a concerning trend: people dedicate fewer resources to the things they once considered most important.

---

[41] Yahoo Finance. https://finance.yahoo.com/news/jeff-bezos-says-overnight-success-164517288.html

There is really no alternative to developing a strong compass and relentlessly staying true to it under all circumstances. This is where our family and the "culture we have built" as a family becomes important. In my case, some of the best investment ideas came from my son while on a vacation, a source I never imagined and least expected.

So, pack your bags and take your loved ones on vacation for conversations that can change and elevate the quality of life and your overall well-being.

Rx for Relax. Onto Prescription No. 3

Chapter 15

Prescription 3: Shifting Mindsets

"The ability to observe without evaluating is the highest form of intelligence." – Jiddu Krishnamurti

As a doctor, you have trained yourself to rely on your instincts and the large vocabulary of insights and knowledge gained from your experience. When there is an emergency, and you are faced with imminent morbidity or possible mortality, the doctors' instinct kicks in almost exactly like a high-performance athlete. You can anticipate the trajectory of the disease in your patients, like a Federer, who could anticipate where the tennis ball will be returned.

Doctors, given their training, practice, and situations, are trained to move swiftly and behave like high-performance athletes. This instinct and capability is embedded into their psyche and is second nature. And it suits and works well for the doctor and their patients. Senior doctors make decisions that are immediately carried out. Things happen quickly, and bureaucracy in implementing decisions is not an option. There are no "endless" debates and discussions.

That is, until they meet with the hospital administration. Everything slows down, and the management board room seems like a "time warp." The doctor might very well feel like entering a parallel and a strange alien universe, where everything seems to move in "slow motion".

Administrators deal with complicated and sometimes even frustrating bureaucracy. Decisions can be centralized, and multiple approvals may be required before a decision can be implemented. Management decisions have implications for people's roles and security. There is no telling how each individual or group might respond. Several stakeholders within the hospital ecosystem have conflicting agendas and goals. Any decision therefore must be carefully weighed and calibrated.

Much financial, scenario, and sensitivity analysis might be needed. This may take time and require more board approval. Doctors probably wonder why a decision to improve good outcomes requires endless meetings and time.

This contrast between cultures in the "procedure room" and the "board room" may partially explain the reasons for conflict and the frustrations that doctors might experience with administration and vice versa. So, what can doctors do?

I prescribe the following recommendation: Shift Mindset.

1. Reflect: Could the instinct that the doctor developed within their clinical practice probably come in the way when engaging with the administration? Could this be the case of two contrasting worlds colliding?

2. If yes, then disarm administration and management!

3. As a doctor, when you walk towards the admin wing (which is generally characterized by carpeted floors and generously upholstered interiors with the constant whiff of coffee and suited men and women twiddling their pens, sitting around polished mahogany oval tables), adopt a different attitude. Change Gears. Change Mindset. Adopt an almost Zen-like attitude.

4. Consciously move away from what is "natural" and instinctive to you. To a mental state that is more "deliberate," "calibrated," and "computative." A colder, more measured approach, a process that is trained to look at statistics and numbers. Put on a Poker face. Disarm the board, by admitting the efforts you are making towards contributing better to the board.

Remember, that managers can never do what doctors can. But doctors can equip themselves to do theirs or at least influence them. Also, every dollar of revenue that a hospital makes is a direct result of the doctors' decisions on patient care plans. Hospitals are and will always be about doctors and patients. Not operations managers, finance controllers, strategic advisors, and other bean counters.

To help doctors make this shift in mindset, I would like to lean on the seminal work of Nobel Laureate Prof. Daniel Kahneman. His book "Thinking, Fast and Slow" is a masterpiece. His contributions to behavioral economics and utility theory are significant and far-reaching. I would strongly recommend getting a copy if you haven't already.

There is no substitute for reading the book and adopting the strategies Kahneman recommends. However, I will try to provide a brief outline of parts of the book that are relevant to this chapter on Mindset.

Prof. Kahneman introduces the idea of System 1 (I call it Automatic Thinking Process or ATP) and System 2 (I call it Deliberate Thinking Process or DTP) thinking. Please look at Exhibit 15.1.

Due to the reasons I indicated at the beginning of the chapter, I assume that doctors might naturally reside in System 1 or ATP. Due to their insights and knowledge of human anatomy and disease progression, most doctors' System 1/ATP is also integrated with a strong intuition that is based on a large vocabulary of knowledge. However, when it comes to matters like management and economics, a doctor may not have the same capability. Therefore, moving away from System 1/ATP is a possible remedy. Let me make my argument by explaining the differences between ATP and DTP.

SHIFT IN THINKING

	ATP*	DTP**
Brain Location	Limbic system	Neocortex
Velocity	Fast	Slow
Thinking Type	Intuitive	Rational
	Qualitative	Scientific
	Pattern	Deliberate
Decision Type	Simple	Complex
Conscious State	Unconscious	Conscious
Effort Level	Lower	Higher
Error Rate	Higher	Lower
Characteristic	Associative	Analytical
Advantage	Fast	Accurate
Disadvantage	Biased	Slow

AUTOMATIC VS DELIBERATE THINKING

SYSTEM 1 - ATP
- Substitutes easy questions for hard ones
- Believes things that are easy to believe

SYSTEM 2 - DTP
- Does the job properly but uses a lot of glucose

Exhibit 15.1: System 1 v/s System 2 Thinking. Courtesy: Prof. D. Kahneman, Thinking, Fast and Slow
*ATP-Automatic Thinking Process. **DTP-Deliberate Thinking Process

1. ATP or System 1 resides and emanates from the Limbic System or Emotional Brain. DTP or System 2 resides and emanates from the Neo-Cortex or the Rational/Thinking Brain.

2. ATP or System 1 is quick and efficient, but it is also very shallow and could be erroneous, whereas System 2 is inefficient and slow but also more accurate.

3. ATP/System1 thought processes are generally more qualitative and intuitive, whereas DTP/System 2 is more scientific and rational. Sometimes, intuition can be overrated and must be tested against available data.

4. ATP/System 1 is more pattern-oriented, whereas DTP/Sys 2 is more deliberate. This could lead ATP to become overconfident when dealing with similar patterns and might decide without adequate investigation. As an example, one danger for doctors is jumping quickly to a diagnosis based on symptoms when a thorough examination could reveal a completely different diagnosis. The biases we might have are generally rooted in System 1/ATP, and this is something doctors should be wary of.

5. ATP/System 1 is fast and generally unconscious, requiring no effort, whereas DTP/System 2 is conscious, requiring a lot more effort and using up a lot of glucose.

The biggest danger and disadvantage of System 1 is that it makes us vulnerable to our Biases and Prejudices. There are no active quality assurance or vigilance functions that check System 1 or ATP thinking and its output.

This can be quite dangerous when complex situations confront us, whether clinically or organizationally. As doctors, there is a high likelihood that their System 2/DTP is relatively weaker than their System 1/ATP. This is just a hypothesis and I'm purely basing it on my observations and experiences.

The ability of doctors to alter their mindset and activate their System 2 thinking could be an important weapon in their armory. Especially as doctors are called upon to lead and influence key organizational decisions and policies.

But are doctors, reluctant leaders?

When confronted with the offer of taking up a role in management and leadership, I have generally sensed a hesitation. Even reluctance. For many doctors, accepting a leadership role requires, as it does for most leaders, a personal transformation – a change in their self-concept and a shift in mindset. Shift like the one we just discussed.

I, however, wonder if there were more mundane and practical concerns at play that causes this apparent reluctance among doctors. Below are some that come to my mind:

1. Would getting involved in management dilute or compromise my clinical skills and capabilities? Won't I lose touch and fall behind?

2. Isn't being a doctor more prestigious than being a manager?

3. Would getting into management dilute my earnings?

4. My training hasn't provided me with adequate background in strategy, economics, leadership, performance management, negotiations, dealing with boards, etc.

These are valid concerns. However, the dynamics and trends with regulation and technology worldwide, leave doctors little choice. But they have an ace up their sleeve, which they may have forgotten about. Doctors forget that, partly due to their training and vocation, they have an edge over other professionals. Doctors naturally tend to be lifelong learners. They generally continue to develop the capability and capacity to handle the unknown, the uncertain, the unpredictable, the volatile, the ambiguous, and the emergent. This, given the nature of our biology and the constant changes in medical science.

If they can harness this natural strength and make the mindset shift, they will be in a unique position to offer what is so desperately needed in hospitals:

1. Negotiating Good Compromises

2. Embracing creative and collaborative models

The final pages of this journey ends with a glimpse of Dr. AI and doctors' current attitude towards economics and lawsuits.

Section 4

Afterthoughts

Chapter 16

Dr. AI will see you now!

"AI won't replace doctors, but doctors who use AI will replace those who don't." – Dr. Eric Topol

House, the Golden Globes, and Emmy award-winning medical drama series created by David Shore is one of my favorites. The main character Dr. Gregory House often disregards medical protocols and uses his brilliant intuition to diagnose and solve complex medical cases. I met a Dr. House-like doctor during my cancer treatment. Post a radical and complex surgery, I had a condition that perplexed my doctors. The condition was acute and most of the attending physicians seemed clueless. One evening, they invited the chief of surgery to examine me. Within minutes he exclaimed, "I know what this is" and then went on to deliver a series of meds and interventions I needed. Miraculously my body responded, and I felt like a patient in one of the House series.

I started to think, how do these great medical minds think. What sets them apart? Are they somehow gifted or is there a method to their brilliant intuitions?

Typically, doctors would use the following steps to narrow down the possible diagnoses for a condition:

1. Patient History

2. Physical Exam

3. Facts about condition and complaint

4. Preliminary tests and questions

5. Arrive at "Differential Diagnosis"

6. Assign "weights" to symptoms, history, exposure

7. Narrow down suspects

8. Order lab tests, imaging

9. Confirm hypothesis and seal diagnosis

However, how would a character or a brilliant medical mind like Dr. House diagnose? He would ask the patient to demonstrate a symptom, then roll out a few adjectives and a few more invectives. And then spit out 2-3 possible causes. He might steth the patient, observe him closely and proclaim his diagnosis. Tests are ordered which usually confirm the diagnosis of the medical magician.

It turns out that brains of brilliant minds in medicine as in other fields don't apply the "rule book" to the images or tests. They apply "pattern recognition". They probably have a strong "knowledge vocabulary" that allows them to "see" patterns that normal doctors miss or are unable to do. Enter Dr. AI.

There is no better pattern recognition engine than a well-trained AI model. I can potentially hire such an AI model for a few cents/dollars and diagnose pretty much myself without the need of going to a crowded hospital that seems like a zoo, (only more chaotic) to stand in queue for hours only to meet a junior doctor, who barely speaks to me and just orders tests. If I could ask the right questions and provide my AI model the right prompts, I might receive reasonably good diagnosis (with the standard disclaimers). This is possible today. Imagine, with the acceleration in compute power and the $1 Trillion investment, the situation within 15-20 years of this writing. AI and technology will completely disrupt medicine, and the way doctors work and operate. AI models are incredibly more powerful pattern recognition engines than humans can ever be.

Think about this situation: I could theoretically ingest a neural network with 10,00,000 case studies of melanoma in little time. How much time do you think a human being who intends to study dermatology will take to pore over and understand 100 cases of melanoma, let alone 1 million case studies. I can do the same for breast cancer, cardiovascular disease, and all the rest of it. Not only these cases, but I could also feed into this AI model (that trains itself) more corpus from medical literature like associated genomics, microbiomes, proteomics, and the rest of it. Imagine the power of such a system to provide accurate, personalized, precise diagnostics and treatment options. For example, our current ability to predict the future risk of breast cancer is primarily based on the presence of highly penetrant gene combinations like BrCa1 and BrCa2. Imagine what an AI model that has been ingested with multiple sources of data can do with the possibility of accurate predictions. AI systems are orthogonal and additive. Qualities that are almost impossible for humans. For example, today we rely on remarkably wasteful levels of mammography that have a high false-positive rate and read by poorly trained mammographers. Imagine the change a well-trained AI system can bring to this and all allied areas of diagnostics and medicine.

AI will disrupt in ways we cannot even imagine now. In my personal life, I now don't rely on secretaries, legal assistants and so many other tasks that I would depend on a human being for earlier. And AI is never late and there are no excuses of a mother or uncle being ill or admitted in a hospital etc. Or wanting a salary advance or a raise. AI will make a lot of jobs irrelevant[42].

---

[42] Goldman Sachs Report: Exploding Topics. AI replacing jobs: A complete overview.

Some estimate that AI could eliminate about 25-30% of all the jobs being performed today by human beings[43]. As an example, today, I may need people like a maid or a driver, who I hire but I can probably exploit. Give them lower wages and not adequate benefits, etc. But with AI, several hordes of jobs could just become irrelevant. This in the future could include managers, CEO's and even some doctors. I wonder if it is safer to be a nurse than a doctor in an AI-driven world. This is a dystopian view, and many disagree with me. And understandably so.

Contrastingly, many argue that AI will, in the future, make medicine more humanistic. It will allow for more time together between doctors and patients. To cultivate and restore trust and pursue the best options for a better quality of life. This could also be true. In my experience 60-70% of the doctors are open and welcoming of AI into their day-to-day workflow.

The jury is still out, and I wonder how this will unfold. My view remains a tad dystopian. Human intelligence is not going to change much, but machines are going to get way smarter, way faster. So, do you still want to see Dr. AI? He is waiting!

---

[43] McKinsey & Company Analysis: McKinsey Global Institute. (2023). Generative AI and the future of work in America.

Chapter 17

Doctors, Economics & Lawsuits

"In the business of healthcare, the patient is the product, not the customer."

There is an extremely high degree of information and knowledge asymmetry. Between the doctor and the patient. Also, between the doctor and the insurer. This asymmetry could potentially allow the doctor to manipulate the medical relationship either with the patient or the insurer.

Another aspect of microeconomics that is particularly relevant to healthcare is the idea of "Induced Demand." In most cases, the doctor is both the producer and consumer. The doctor translates the patient's medical condition (demand) into a medical consumption (by deciding the care plan and prescriptions). This makes the doctor all too powerful. Despite advances in technology and the availability of online AI tools, patients will always remain uncertain and generally cannot protect themselves from poor quality of care or poor diagnosis.

Healthcare is also seen as a "social good." The existence of social obligations prevents the doctor from behaving like an over-eager car dealership salesperson. Can we continue to count on this innate goodness of doctors?

Most doctors are part of large healthcare systems that are predominantly fee-for-service. Despite all rhetoric about compassion and care for patients, shareholder objectives will always trump patient objectives every single time. And that is understandable. However, what safety nets can patients rely on?

My sentiment, when I'm admitted into a hospital, is: "I may genuinely distrust this hospital system, but I tend to trust the doctor who I am admitted under. I just hope that he/she will do the right thing by me". This means that I should somehow know the odds of the doctor doing the right thing. How is that possible?

How can I examine if my assumption of the doctor is accurate? Luckily for me, I stumbled upon a study conducted by Johns Hopkins[44]. It gives us a glimpse into doctors' attitudes towards economics generally. Not a direct answer but a proxy. Especially in the absence of any other study that I could find that would help examine my assumption.

The survey invited 3,318 physicians to participate with questions concerning their healthcare practices. This was later published, and the results are summarized below:

1. Barely 7% of the doctors expressed enthusiasm for "eliminating" fee-for-service payment models. They seem to be happy with a model that keeps paying them and the hospital for doing more stuff. Without much accountability for outcomes.

2. Almost 60% of the doctors put the onus on health insurance companies and hospitals to be "majorly responsible" for reducing healthcare costs.

3. Physicians believe overtreatment is common and primarily perpetuated by fear of malpractice, as well as patient demand and some profit motives.

4. Only 36% reported that practicing physicians have a "major responsibility" for reducing costs.

---

[44] Lyu, H., Xu, T., Brotman, D., Mayer-Blackwell, B., Cooper, M., Daniel, M., & Makary, M. A. (2017). Overtreatment in the United States. PloS one, 12(9), e0181970.

5. However, 89% felt that "doctors need to take a more prominent role in limiting the use of unnecessary tests"

6. 78% felt that they "should be solely devoted to individual patients' best interests, even if that is expensive."

7. 79% agreed they should adhere to clinical guidelines that discourage the use of marginally beneficial care.

8. 76% of physicians reported being "aware of the costs" of the tests/treatments they recommend.

The survey results momentarily dented my assumptions and confidence about my doctors. I couldn't help but notice the dichotomy and hypocrisy in the doctors' responses when it comes to reducing costs and their own roles in it. Traditionally, the doctor has been "paternalistic." Under whose care the patients "submit" and cooperate willingly like obedient children. The doctor is seen as a benevolent dictator who knows what is good for the patient (like the "good father"). The doctor's "happiness" is a derivative of a cured and "happy" patient. The "paternalistic" power is regulated by the sense of responsibility in doctors. This is OK by me, when it is just me and my doctor. But now, we are both immersed in a complex and turbulently violent ecosystem. Most doctors, however, do the right thing and always try to do so. This I know.

In conclusion, the recent spurt in medico-legal cases, is a matter of some concern for doctors. Concern because much of it doesn't quite accurately reflect the doctor's situation and context but also because it encourages doctors to practice more "defensive" medicine, which drives up costs. It is also unfair for a sincere, hard-working, and conscientious doctor to feel vulnerable to litigation and that somehow affecting his/her performance.

Decades-old studies[45] have shown that primary care physicians are sued way less than their tertiary counterparts. I'm not sure you noticed, but our GP's and primary care doctors are usually more accessible and relatively friendlier. They tend to do a lot of "small talk" and PR that patients seem to like and enjoy. They spend time educating patients and more likely to laugh with patients and their relatives. They also tend to encourage patients to talk and express their opinions. Maybe the more likable, cordial and charming physicians are, the less likely they are sued. Could it be that simple?

A study published in 1989 surveyed patients who sued physicians as well as physicians who had or had not been sued. Patients who sued and Doctors who were sued disagreed on just about everything, except one area. A vast majority of the surveyed doctors and patients (almost 70%) thought that improved communication could reduce malpractice litigation.

Exhibit 17.1 captures the essence of the study.

---

[45] Shapiro, R. S., Simpson, D. E., Lawrence, S. L., Talsky, A. M., Sobocinski, K. A., & Schiedermayer, D. L. (1989).

DOCTORS AND LAWSUITS

Only 20% of patients reported financial compensation as their motive for suing. However, 80% of all physicians thought this was the reason patients filed suits.

A study published in 1989 surveyed patients who sued physicians as well as physicians who had or had not been sued.

Only 10% of the physicians sued, thought negligence was the reason for claims against them.

Almost all (97%) of the patients reported negligence as the reason for their malpractice action.

About 70% of both groups, doctors and patients, thought that improved communication could reduce future malpractice litigation.

Exhibit 17.1: Doctors and Lawsuits. Courtesy: Adapted from Robyn Shapiro, JAMA'89

The message for doctors is clear. If you don't want to be sued, Listen More and Laugh Often!!!

References and Notes

1. Advisory Board. (2024, April 16). Physician employment trends: PAI and Avalere study findings

2. Reifferscheid, P., Morin, P., & Wasem, J. (2014). Umgang mit Mittelknappheit im Krankenhaus. Springer-Verlag.

3. Medscape. (2024). Medscape physician lifestyle & burnout report.

4. Duarte, D., El-Hagrassy, M. M., Couto, T. C. E., Gurgel, W., Fregni, F., & Correa, H. (2020). Physician suicide: A systematic review and meta-analysis. PLOS ONE, 15(12), e0226361.

5. National Transportation Safety Board (NTSB). Directorate General of Civil Aviation (DGCA).

6. Why 70 percent of physicians would not recommend the profession. (2018). Healthcare Finance News.

7. Makary, M. A., & Daniel, M. (2016). Medical error—the third leading cause of death in the US. BMJ, 353, i2139.

8. World Health Organization. (2019). Patient safety: Global action on patient safety.

9. Bloomberg Media. (2022).

10. Kahneman, D. (2011). Thinking, fast and slow. Farrar, Straus and Giroux.

11. Hamel, G. (2013). The Morning Star Company: Self-management at work (Case No. 914-013). Harvard Business School

12. BBC. (2013, September 23). Valve: How going boss-free empowers staff.

13. Research-Methodology. (n.d.). Amazon organizational structure: A brief overview.

14. Reason, J. (1990). Human error. Cambridge University Press.

15. Investopedia. (n.d.). How to talk to kids about money—and why you should do so early.

16. Yahoo Finance. https://finance.yahoo.com/news/jeff-bezos-says-overnight-success-164517288.html

17. Author Notes. This is only a reference and can vary widely depending on the city, type, size, and medical program of the hospital. Applies mainly to emerging economies.

18. Operating leverage is a financial concept that measures the proportion of fixed costs in a company's cost structure. It indicates how a change in sales volume will affect a

company's operating income due to the presence of fixed costs in its operations. The higher the operating leverage, the more a company's profits can increase with additional sales because fixed costs remain constant as sales increase. A tertiary care hospital with high operating leverage will see a more significant impact on profitability from changes in patient volume. If patient volume increases, the hospital can spread its fixed costs over a larger number of patients, potentially increasing profitability.

19. In the context of operating leverage and business risk, contribution refers to the contribution margin, which is the amount remaining from sales revenue after deducting variable costs. This margin contributes to covering fixed costs and generating profit.

20. EBIT-earnings before interest and taxes. EBT-earnings before taxes.

21. Operating Leverage (OL): OL = Contribution Margin / EBIT. Financial Leverage (FL): FL = EBIT / EBT. Combined Leverage (CL): CL = OL × FL = Contribution Margin / EBT

22. Rauscher, S., & Wheeler, J. R. C. (2012). The importance of working capital management for hospital profitability. Rauscher, S., & Wheeler, J. R. C. (2012). The importance of working capital management for hospital profitability: Evidence from bond-issuing, not-for-profit U.S. hospitals. Health Care Management Review, 37(4), 339-346.

23. Veronesi, G., Kirkpatrick, I., & Vallascas, F. (2013). Clinicians on the board: What difference does it make? BMC Health Services Research, 13, 424.

24. Capital Asset Pricing Model (CAPM)

25. Ho, V., & Jenkins, D. (2024, October 21). Hospital price increases since 2000 outpaced inflation by more than double, Baker Institute report says. Rice University's Baker Institute for Public Policy.

26. "Our Story":Aravind Eye Care System. (n.d.).

27. Profit & Loss

28. Kilic, A., Acker, M. A., Gleason, T. G., Sultan, I., Vemulapalli, S., Thibault, D., & Kilic, A. (2019). Clinical outcomes of mitral valve reoperations in the United States: an analysis of the Society of Thoracic Surgeons National Database. The Annals of thoracic surgery, 107(3), 754-759

29. Kaplan, R. S., & Witkowski, M. L. (2014). Using time-driven activity-based costing to identify value-improvement opportunities in healthcare. Journal of Healthcare Management, 59(6), 399-413.

30. Institute for Strategy and Competitiveness. (n.d.). Measure outcomes & cost for every patient. Harvard Business School.

31. Feldman, L. S., Shihab, H. M., Thiemann, D., Yeh, H. C., Ardolino, M., Mandell, S., & Brotman, D. J. (2013). Impact of providing fee data on laboratory test ordering: A controlled clinical trial. JAMA Internal Medicine, 173(10), 903-908.

32. Mann School of Pharmacy and Pharmaceutical Sciences. (n.d.). USC study reveals strategy to save $70 million in health care. University of Southern California.

33. Appleby, J. (2021, February 10). How much does a C-section cost at one hospital? Anywhere from $6,241 to $60,584. The Wall Street Journal.

34. Mathews, A. W., McGinty, T., & Evans, M. (2021, February 10). How much does a C-section cost? The Wall Street Journal. Feb 11, 2021

35. Mathews, A. W., McGinty, T., & Evans, M. (2021, February 10). How much does a C-section cost? The Wall Street Journal. Feb 11, 2021

36. Chernew, M. E., Dafny, L. S., & Pany, M. J. (2020, March 10). A proposal to cap provider prices and price growth in the commercial health-care market. Brookings Institution.

37. Ly, D. P., & Cutler, D. M. (2018). Factors of U.S. hospitals associated with improved profit margins: An observational study. Journal of General Internal Medicine, 33(7), 1020-1027.

38. Centers for Medicare & Medicaid Services. (2021). Hospital price transparency overview. U.S. Department of Health & Human Services.

39. The American Medical Association (AMA) releases a series of Policy Research Perspectives that examine methods, such as salary and productivity, used to compensate physicians. Readers interested in a deep dive can visit the AMA website. It is a fascinating read.

40. HeyInfluent. (n.d.). Employed vs private practice: Pros and cons.

41. Porter, M. E. (2010). What is value in health care? The New England Journal of Medicine, 363(26), 2477-2481.

42. I highly recommend googling ICOHM. It has defined and published over 12 global standards for outcomes measurement so far.

43. Goldman Sachs Report: Exploding Topics. (n.d.). AI replacing jobs: A complete overview.

44. *McKinsey & Company Analysis: McKinsey Global Institute.* (2023). Generative AI and the future of work in America.

45. Lyu, H., Xu, T., Brotman, D., Mayer-Blackwell, B., Cooper, M., Daniel, M., & Makary, M. A. (2017). Overtreatment in the United States. PloS one, 12(9), e0181970.

46. Shapiro, R. S., Simpson, D. E., Lawrence, S. L., Talsky, A. M., Sobocinski, K. A., & Schiedermayer, D. L. (1989).

Share your thoughts on this book and stay connected through my social media channels:

LinkedIn: https://www.linkedin.com/in/sudhakarjayaram/
YouTube: https://www.youtube.com/@sudhakarjayaram819
Patreon: patreon.com/SJai27

Feel free to reach out, ask questions, or engage in discussions related to the book. Let the conversation begin...